Dismissal Law in the Netherlands: A Practical Guide

Dismissal Law in the Netherlands: A Practical Guide

Mirjam A. de Blécourt

eleven international publishing

Published, sold and distributed by Eleven International Publishing
P.O. Box 85576
2508 CG The Hague
The Netherlands
Tel.: +31 70 33 070 33
Fax: +31 70 33 070 30
e-mail: sales@budh.nl
www.elevenpub.com

Sold and distributed in USA and Canada
International Specialized Book Services
920 NE 58th Avenue, Suite 300
Portland, OR 97213-3786, USA
Tel.: 1-800-944-6190 (toll-free)
Fax: +1-503-280-8832
orders@isbs.com
www.isbs.com

Eleven International Publishing is an imprint of Boom uitgevers Den Haag.

ISBN 978-94-6236-650-3

Printed in The Netherlands

Contents

Preface

On 1 July this year (2015), our dismissal law was radically amended and laid down in the Dutch Work and Security Act (*Wet Werk en Zekerheid* (*Wwz*)). 'Dismissal law must become simpler, fairer, faster and cheaper.'[1] These are the words the social partners have always used after concluding the social agreement to explain why the law had to change. As I write, it is October 2015 and a picture is forming that many, including myself, had anticipated.

Dismissing employees has not become easier and in most cases not cheaper either. For SMEs it is now even more expensive. Whereas those employers usually did not pay dismissal compensation in the event of individual dismissals before 1 July 2015, under the Wwz they have to pay transition compensation. Also for collective dismissals, where negotiations have to be held with trade unions about a social plan, dismissal is much more expensive than the transition compensation.[2] Under the Wwz, derogation from transition compensation is allowed in a social plan. The trade unions view transition compensation as an absolute minimum. They have even called for strikes in cases in which the employer offered transition compensation as an opening bid. Also, transition compensation does not apply in individual cases if

1 *Parliamentary Papers II* 2013/14, 33818, no. 3, p. 5.

2 See the social plans of Aegon Nederland 1 July 2015 - 1 July 2018, Teijin Aramid B.V. 1 July 2015 - 1 July 2018, Telegraaf Media Groep N.V. 1 July 2015 - 1 December 2015 and V&D B.V. and La Place B.V. 1 July 2015 - 1 February 2016.

the employer wants to end employment amicably. The employer will have to offer more than transition compensation in order to get the employee to agree to his/her dismissal. The sub-district court formula, which applied before 1 July 2015, is usually offered.

Just before the Wwz was introduced, there was a rise in collective dismissals. Up to the end of June 2015, the Employee Insurance Agency (*Uitvoeringsinstituut Werknemersverzekeringen* (UWV)) granted 10,500 dismissal permits, 77% of which were granted for business economic reasons. Social plans were still concluded up to the end of June 2015, with compensation based on the sub-district court formula (which amounted to about three times as much as the transition compensation).[3] In June, 4,900 dismissal applications were submitted to the UWV. This is almost twice as many as in May.[4] As far as we can tell in our practice, this spate of dismissals has not slowed down since 1 July.

After all the government's assertions about the new Act being 'simpler, fairer, faster and cheaper', how do you explain to the General Legal Counsel, the HR director or the CEO of a company that the Act has not made things cheaper and certainly not simpler? Moreover, how do you explain that the transitional compensation included in the Wwz is not compensation that the trade unions will agree to in a social plan? In October 2014 it was already posted on the website of the National Federation of Chris-

3 See 'Developments in the sub-district court formula in social plans', April 2015. Consult via www.awvn.nl.

4 UWV, 'Nieuwsflits Arbeidsmarkt Juni 2015', 16 July 2015, p. 9, http://www.uwv.nl/overuwv/kennis-cijfers-en-onderzoek/arbeidsmarktinformatie/nieuwsflits-arbeidsmarkt-juni-2015.aspx.

tian Trade Unions in the Netherlands (CNV) that the trade unions would not agree to the transition budget in social plans.[5] Other trade unions also took the position that they can request the old sub-district court formula, because there is, after all, freedom of contract.[6] That puzzled businesses, because the trade unions, as did the Confederation of Netherlands Industry and Employers (VNO-NCW), had sat round the table with the government to reach the social agreement on the Wwz.

I was faced with the following question: how do you make it clear at a glance that dismissal law has become anything but simpler? The answer came to me quickly, but the implementation in addition to our busy practices took a lot of time. It became the dismissal poster (WWZ.nl).

Our employment law department, together with Dr W.H.A.C.M. Bouwens, LLM, Professor of Law, and Dr D.M.A. Bij de Vaate, LLM, of the Vrije Universiteit Amsterdam, made a poster on which all the steps that have to be taken by the employer on dismissal are illustrated in a diagram. We are very grateful to Danielle Pinedo, who made a major contribution to this. The design was provided by David Gall and Marco Stout of Spot Infographics. Boom uitgeverij published the dismissal poster (see www.wwzposter.nl). The poster was shown to Minister Lodewijk Asscher on 30 June 2015, the transitional night from the old to the new dismissal law, during a major conference organised by the VAAN. The Minister even asked during

5 http://cnvvakmensen.nl/wie-we-zijn/nieuws/werkgevers-moeten-zich-niet-rijk-rekenen-met-transitievergoeding.

6 http://fd.nl/economie-politiek/1110047/bonden-willen-nog-steeds-hoge-exitpremies-in-sociaal-plan-regelen.

his speech if he could take the poster home. That night the poster was distributed to 1,700 lawyers specialising in employment law. Lectures are given at the VU University Amsterdam on the basis of this poster.

This book is a handy manual for everyone who will be faced with the new dismissal law. The text is supplemented by several clear diagrams that are derived from the poster.

I would like to thank the employment department of Baker & McKenzie Amsterdam, Sharon Looden and Sophie Smeets for their helpful comments on this book.

Mirjam A. de Blécourt
Head Employment & Pensions Law - Baker & McKenzie Amsterdam

Chapter 1
Options for terminating employment contracts

1.1 Introduction

Dutch employment law, including dismissal law, was amended radically in 2015. The Work and Security Act ('Wwz') was introduced in phases at a rapid pace – within a year the legislative proposal had been submitted to the Lower House.[7] Various amendments to Dutch employment law entered into force on 1 January 2015. As of 1 July 2015, dismissal law was reformed in its entirety. This book will deal with the new dismissal law.[8]

An employment contract for an indefinite period of time or for a fixed term with an early termination option can be terminated with or without written consent from the employee. There are two variants of written consent from the employee. First of all, the employee can consent in writing to the termination of his/her employment contract by the employer.[9] The second variant is termination

7 *Bulletin of Acts and Decrees (Staatsblad)* 2014, 216 and *Bulletin of Acts and Decrees* 2014, 504.

8 See also on this subject: W.H.A.C.M. Bouwens & D.M.V. Bij de Vaate, 'Voorwaardelijke procedures in het nieuwe dismissalrecht', *ARBAC* April 2015, DOI:10.5553/ARBAC/221187802015000002001.

9 See *Parliamentary Papers II* 2013/14, 33818, no. 3, pp. 25-26.

of the employment contract by mutual consent. If the employee does not agree to his/her dismissal – depending on the reason for dismissal – the employer can either request the sub-district court to set aside the employment contract or request permission from the Employee Insurance Agency [*Uitvoeringsinstituut Werknemersverzekering* (UWV)] to terminate the employment. In specific, special situations, or if a special person is being dismissed, such preventive review by either the UWV or the sub-district court is not necessary if the employee does not agree to his/her dismissal. This then concerns:

1. dismissal during the probationary period;
2. summary dismissal;
3. dismissal during insolvency;
4. dismissal of a director/officer of a legal entity other than a foundation;
5. dismissal of an employee in a ministry;
6. dismissal of an employee who has reached state pension age or a different retirement age;
7. dismissal of a domestic service provider;
8. dismissal of an employee at a privately run school or institution due to acts or omissions incompatible with its religious or philosophical identity and for which permission for termination was granted by an impartial committee independent of the employer.

Dutch employment law is confusing, particularly for foreign clients. As an illustration: an American employer reads in the employment contract with his employee that the employment contract can be terminated with a notice period of two months. How could he know that the law requires all kinds of steps to be taken for such a termination? He writes a letter to the employee that he is terminating the employment contract, is observing the notice period and that the employment contract will therefore end in two months. He does not realise that in the Netherlands a preventive review of the reason for dismissal must take place if the employee does not agree to his/her dismissal.

In the following, the aforementioned possibilities for the employer to terminate an indefinite employment contract (or for a fixed term with an early termination option) is dealt with step by step.[10]

Different rules apply to termination of an employment contract for a fixed term without an early termination option. These will be dealt with separately in Section 1.5.[11]

1.2 The employee agrees in writing to termination of his/her employment contract

1.2.1 Termination by mutual consent (Book 7, Section 670b of the Dutch Civil Code (*Burgerlijk Wetboek* (BW)))

An employment contract can be terminated by mutual consent. No notice of termination by the employer is

10 Dismissal during insolvency, dismissal of an employee in a ministry, dismissal of a domestic servant and dismissal of an employee at a privately run school or institution due to acts or omissions incompatible with its religious or philosophical identity and for which permission was granted by an impartial committee independent of the employer will not be dealt with in this book.

11 The termination of an employment contract at the employee's request will not be taken into consideration in this handbook. See as an example for termination at the employee's request: *Parliamentary Papers II* 2013/14, 33818, no. 3, p. 33.

required for this and the employer and employee can determine themselves for what reason and under what conditions they are to part company. Such termination must take place in writing, otherwise the agreement will not be valid according to Book 7, Section 670b subsection 1 BW. If the employee agrees to a proposal for termination by mutual consent, he/she has not become 'culpably unemployed' by signing the termination or other agreement (Section 24 subsections 2 and 6 of the Dutch Unemployment Insurance Act [*Werkloosheidswet* (WW)]). Consequently, the employee will not lose any claim to unemployment benefits. If the employer and employee conclude a written termination agreement, the employee will not have a right to transition compensation (Book 7, Section 673 BW).

1.2.1.a 'Right of reflection'

If the employee has signed the termination agreement, under Book 7, Section 670b subsection 2 BW he/she will have the right to cancel the termination agreement within 14 days after the date on which the termination agreement was concluded, without stating reasons, by way of a written statement addressed to the employer.[12] The employer must draw the employee's attention to this possibility in the termination agreement. If the employer does not point it out in writing, the reflection time will be extended by a week to become three weeks (Book 7, Section 670b subsection 3 BW). Our government considered it desirable to provide the employee with extra protection

12 This does not apply to a director or officer under the articles of association; see Book 7, Section 670b subsection 5 BW.

in this way.[13] Any stipulation by which the 'reflection' time is limited or excluded is null and void (Book 7, Section 670b subsection 6 BW). The right of reflection can be invoked only once every six months (Book 7, Section 670b subsection 4 BW).[14]

This reflection time is very impractical in practice. The employer only finds out after two or three weeks have passed whether the deal made will go through. If the employee goes back on the termination agreement, the negotiation process will then start again. Ways will be sought to circumvent the reflection period. One way is to file pro forma setting aside proceedings at the sub-district court on the grounds of c to h, Book 7, Section 669 subsection 3 BW. If the parties agree on termination of the employment contract, the sub-district court will establish the setting aside of the employment contract in a court ruling. In that case this will not count as a termination agreement, so the reflection period will not apply to it. The same holds if the judge sends the employer and employee out of the room during a hearing and then establishes the arrangement they agreed in the court ruling.[15] An agreement concluded to make an arrangement for the so-called loose ends will not count as a termination agreement either within the meaning of Book 7, Section 670b BW.[16]

13 *Parliamentary Papers II* 2013/14, 33818, no. 3, p. 103.

14 *Parliamentary Papers II* 2013/14, 33818, no. 8, p. 17.

15 *Parliamentary Papers II* 2013/14, 33818, no. 3, p. 103.

16 L.G. Verburg, 'Schikken in het nieuwe ontslagrecht: bedenk eer ge begint', *ArA* 2014, 2.

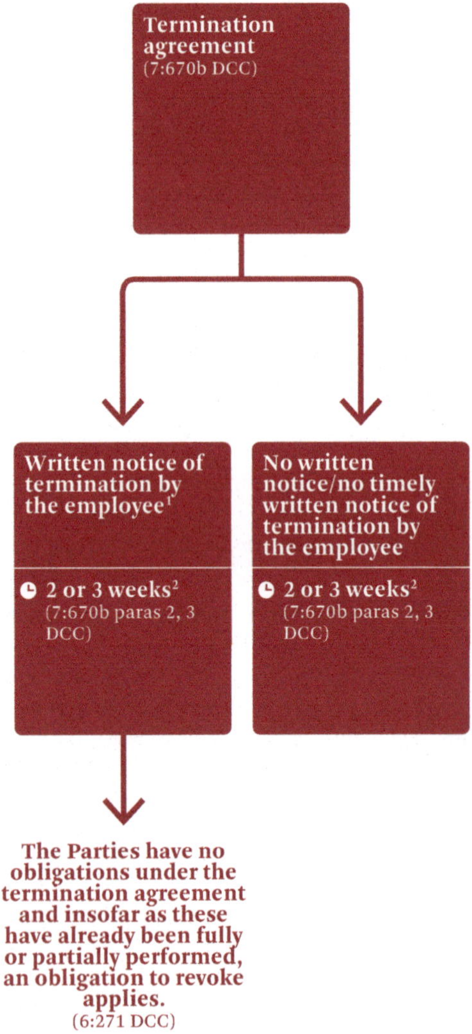
Termination agreement
(7:670b DCC)
Written notice of termination by the employee[1]
2 or 3 weeks[2]
(7:670b paras 2, 3 DCC)
No written notice/no timely written notice of termination by the employee
2 or 3 weeks[2]
(7:670b paras 2, 3 DCC)
The Parties have no obligations under the termination agreement and insofar as these have already been fully or partially performed, an obligation to revoke applies.
(6:271 DCC)

1.2.2 Termination with the employee's written agreement (Book 7, Section 671 BW)

A new dismissal route is termination with the employee's consent. Under Book 7, Section 671 subsection 1 BW, the employer can terminate the employment contract with the employee's written agreement.

According to legistative history, a reasonable ground is also required for termination with the employee's consent.[17] A sanction for the lack of a reasonable ground, however, does not exist.[18] For termination with consent, the employer owes transition compensation (provided the conditions for this have been met: Book 7, Section 673 BW) and if termination has taken place on business economic grounds, the termination can be nullified owing to breach of the condition for recommencement of employment (see Section 2.1.1). It is doubtful if the employee can rely on a special prohibition on termination or non-observance of the notice period by the employer after having agreed to termination (see Section 2.1).[19]

It is still unclear why the government included this possibility, as termination by mutual consent has also been maintained. The latter is more important for the practice, not only because there is no possibility of appeal, which is the case with consent, but also because transition compensation is due for termination with consent,

17 *Parliamentary Papers II* 2013/14, 33818, no. 3, p. 103. See also Section 1.2.2 in this book.

18 See also: E.M. Hoogeveen, 'De opzegging met instemming, de beëindigingsovereenkomst en de bedenktermijn: nieuwe wegen vol valkuilen', *ArbeidsRecht* 2014/48.

19 W.H.A.C.M. Bouwens & R.A.A. Duk, *Van der Grinten Arbeidsovereenkomstenrecht*, Deventer: Kluwer 2015, p. 370.

whereas it is not due if there is a termination agreement. The question is why an employee would agree to termination with consent. He/she is more likely to be tempted to sign a termination agreement that included a higher amount than transition compensation.

1.2.2.a 'Right of reflection'

Under the second subsection of Book 7, Section 671 BW, the employee can revoke his/her agreement within 14 days after the date without stating reasons, by way of a written statement addressed to the employer.[20] If the employer does not draw the employee's attention to the right of reflection in writing within two working days after the agreement was given, the period will become three weeks instead of two (Book 7, Section 671 subsection 3 BW). If the employee revokes his/her agreement in writing in time, the termination will be deemed not to have taken place (Book 7, Section 671 subsection 4 BW).

20 This does not apply to a director or officer under the articles of association. For directors or officers under the articles of association, see Book 7 Section 670a subsection 7 BW. See also: E.M. Hoogeveen, 'De opzegging met instemming, de beëindigingsovereenkomst en de bedenktermijn: nieuwe wegen vol valkuilen', *ArbeidsRecht* 2014/48; L.G. Verburg, 'Schikken in het nieuwe ontslagrecht: bedenk eer ge begint', *ArA* 2014, 2.

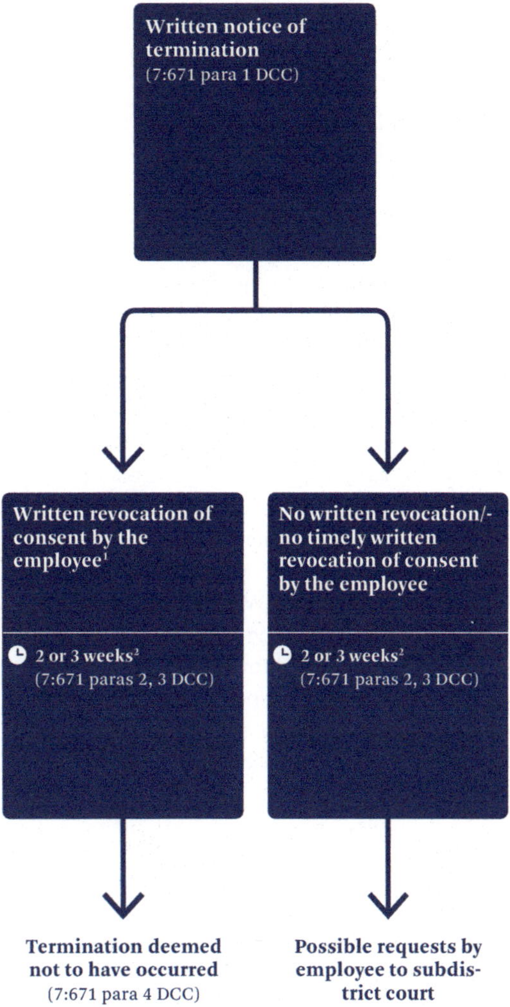
Written notice of termination
(7:671 para 1 DCC)
Written revocation of consent by the employee[1]
2 or 3 weeks[2]
(7:671 paras 2, 3 DCC)
No written revocation/- no timely written revocation of consent by the employee
2 or 3 weeks[2]
(7:671 paras 2, 3 DCC)
Termination deemed not to have occurred
(7:671 para 4 DCC)
Possible requests by employee to subdistrict court

1.3 The employee does not agree in writing to termination of his/her employment contract

1.3.1 Notice of termination and termination in general

Under the Wwz, Book 7, Section 669 BW plays an important role in the termination of an employment contract. This section stipulates that, unless provided otherwise,[21] if the employer wishes to cancel an employment contract, in order to do so:

(i) the employer must have a reasonable ground; and
(ii) if reassignment of the employee within a reasonable period, whether or not with the aid of training, to another suitable job is not possible or is not logical. If the employee has committed imputable acts or (e ground), reassignment is not logical in any case.

In Book 7, Section 669 BW, the words 'notice of termination' are used. It could be concluded from this that this section is not intended for setting aside by the court. In that case, however, grounds c to h, as discussed below, would not belong in this section.[22] This means that the words 'notice of termination' must mean 'setting aside' as well.

21 For example, Book 7, Section 669 BW does not apply to dismissal during the probationary period (see paragraph 7), to dismissal during insolvency, or to summary dismissal, and is not a reasonable ground for dismissal of an employee of state pension or a different retirement age as referred to in Book 7, Section 669 subsection 3 BW (see subsection 4).

22 *Parliamentary Papers II* 2013/14, 33818, no. 3, p. 98.

The third subsection of Book 7, Section 669 BW provides a full list under a to h of the grounds for dismissal that qualify as 'reasonable grounds'.[23] These grounds then determine which route should be chosen for dismissal: termination of the employment contract via the UWV or setting aside by the sub-district court.

Re (i) reasonable grounds for dismissal (Book 7, Section 669 subsection 3 BW)

The reasonable grounds on the basis of which an employment contract can be terminated or setting aside can be requested – listed exhaustively – are the following:

a. Redundancies as a result of discontinuation of the company's operations or the necessary cutting of jobs in a foreseeable period of at least 26 weeks as a result of measures for efficient business operations taken as a consequence of business economic circumstances **(a ground)**. The period of 26 weeks starts on the date on which the request to terminate or set aside the employment contract is submitted.[24]
b. **Employee illness** or disability rendering him or her no longer able to perform the stipulated work, provided the period referred to in Section 670, subsections 1 and 11, has expired and it is plausible that the employee **will not recover within 26 weeks** and that the stipulated work cannot be performed in an adapted form **(b ground)**.

---

23 *Parliamentary Papers II* 2013/14, 33818, no. 3, p. 84 and *Parliamentary Papers II* 2013/14, 33818, no. 7, p. 44.

24 See the explanations to Section 8, Redundancy Regulations (Ontslagregeling), Stcrt. 2015, 12685. p. 14.

c. The employee is **regularly unable to perform the stipulated work as a result of his/her illness** or disability with unacceptable consequences for the business operations (**c ground**).
d. **Unsuitability of the employee for performing the stipulated work**, other than as a result of the employee's illness or disability (**d ground**).
e. **Imputable acts or omissions** on the part of the employee (**e ground**).
f. Refusal by the employee to perform the stipulated work due to **serious conscientious objections (f ground).**
g. A **disrupted employment relationship (g ground).**
h. **Circumstances other than those mentioned above** of such a nature that the employer cannot reasonably be required to allow the employment contract to continue (**h ground**).

Under the Wwz, each reasonable ground must be considered in itself. 'A bit of each ground' will not withstand the reasonable ground test under the Wwz.[25] If the employer has chosen to request the sub-district court to set aside the employment contract on a c to h ground, he/she cannot add business economic reasons as well.[26] I, however, agree with Swelheim when she asserts that there can be several full grounds that can be put forward as alternatives and second alternatives.[27]

25 S.F. Sagel, *Werk en zekerheid: ontslagrecht doen in tijden van hard and fast rules* (Inaugural lecture Leiden).
26 *Parliamentary Papers II* 2013/14, 33818, 3, p. 85 and *Parliamentary Papers I* 2013/14, C, p. 92.
27 A.J. Swelheim, 'Draait de redelijke grond de ontbindingsprocedure op slot?', *ArbeidsRecht* 2014/51.

If an **a or b ground is involved,** under the Wwz a request to terminate the employment contract must then be submitted to the UWV (Book 7, Section 671a BW). For **c to h ground**, the **sub-district court** must be requested to set aside the employment contract (Book 7, Section 671b BW).

Re (ii) reassignment not possible or not logical

Reassignment of the employee to another suitable job with or without the aid of training must not be possible or not logical. Book 7, Section 611a BW prescribes that the employer must enable the employee to take training that is necessary for the performance of his/her job and, in so far as he/she can reasonably be required to do so, for continuation of the employment contract if the employee's job is cut or he/she is no longer able to perform it.

A job is suitable if it is in line with the education, experience and capacities of the employee (Section 9 subsection 3 of the Redundancy Regulations). Pursuant to Section 9 of the Redundancy Regulations, the employer must seek a suitable job within his/her company. If the employer's company is part of a group, it will have to be seen whether a suitable job exists at another company in the group (Section 9 subsection 2 of the Redundancy Regulations).

The duration of the reasonable period is in line with the statutory notice period for dismissal. The period starts on the date that a decision is taken on the UWV request or setting aside of the employment contract.[28]

28 Section 10 subsections 1 and 4 Redundancy Regulations.

1.3.2 Termination by the employer after permission from the UWV or collective bargaining committee on the basis of an a or b ground (Book 7, Section 671a BW)

The employer does not need the employee's consent to terminate the employment contract if one of the following cases referred to in Book 7, Section 671 BW is concerned:

Permission has been given by the UWV or the collective bargaining committee (if provided by a collective labour agreement) to terminate the employment contract on the basis of:

a. **Redundancies** as a result of discontinuation of the company's operations or as a result of business economic circumstances **(a ground)**.
b. **Prolonged illness** of the employee (longer than two years) and recovery within 26 weeks is not likely **(b ground)**.

It may be stipulated in the applicable collective labour agreement that the employer must contact a collective bargaining committee (instead of the UWV) for an a ground. This must be an impartial committee independent of the employer, designated in a collective labour agreement or by or on behalf of the competent executive body. In that case, it is important to read the applicable collective labour agreement to see which route should be followed for termination on an a ground (Book 7, Section 671a subsection 2 BW).

1.3.2.1 Discontinuation of operations or business economic reasons (a ground)

The a ground includes the cutting of jobs as a result of discontinuation of the company's operations or the necessary cutting of jobs over a period to be determined by law as a result of measures taken for effective business operations as a consequence of business economic circumstances. Business economic reasons can be the poor financial position of the company, organisational changes, technological changes, discontinuation of the business operations or reduction of work. Except in case of reduction of work and closure of the business, the employer must demonstrate that there will be structural cutting of jobs. Structural cutting of jobs means a future period of 26 weeks, counting from the date the job(s) expected to be cut. The employer must also make it plausible that the decision on which the cutting of jobs is based is necessary in the interests of effective business operations. That does not apply if the whole company closes. The employer must demonstrate that there are no possibilities for reassignment of the employee to another suitable job, whether or not with the aid of training. Under the new Act, there will be an opportunity for the employer to organise the company in such a way that its continuity is assured in the longer term as well. That is in the interests of preserving jobs in a more general sense. The UWV should therefore exercise somewhat more restraint in reviewing this ground. The UWV will not give permission if employees are presented for dismissal because of a saving on costs that the employer considers necessary (poor financial position), while the nature and scope of the work remain the same. With that, an attempt is made to protect socio-economic relationships in the Netherlands. That balance would be disrupted by the unnecessary replacement of permanent employees by temporary employees and evasion of employer obligations under a collective labour agreement.

If an employer wants to terminate an employment contract because of discontinuation of the operations or for business economic reasons, and if a choice has not been made to terminate the employment contract with the employee's consent or termination of the employment contract by way of a termination agreement, the employer must request permission from the UWV to terminate the employment contract. In its request to the UWV for permission to terminate the employment contract, the employer will have to demonstrate why it is necessary to cut jobs.[29]

To substantiate its request, the employer must provide the UWV with information. This information depends on the business economic reasons given. The information, as is evident from practice, except for reduction of work and closing of the company, can most simply be furnished if the business economic reason is organisational changes.[30] Permission to terminate for business economic reasons will be given only if the substantiation is well founded, no other obvious solutions are possible and not until flex contracts (fixed-term contracts or temporary employment contracts) have been terminated (Book 7, Section 671a subsection 5 BW).[31]

29 *Parliamentary Papers II* 2013/14, 33818, no. 3, p. 43.

30 Part C of the 'Application for a dismissal permit for business economic reasons' form.

31 *Parliamentary Papers II* 2013/14, 33818, no. 3, p. 44.

1.3.2.1.a Reflection principle

The Minister of Social Affairs and Employment laid down more details for the order of dismissals in the Redundancy Regulations.[32] The reflection principle is included in these regulations. Those rules and the reflection principle are not applicable if other rules are included in the collective labour agreement for the order of dismissals.[33]

The reflection principle applies to the cutting of jobs as a starting point to determine which employee will lose his/her job. Concisely stated, the reflection principle divides the employees with exchangeable jobs into age categories as follows: from 15 until 25 years, from 25 until 35 years, from 35 until 45 years, from 45 until 55 years and from 55 years until the age of entitlement to state pension. The employees eligible for dismissal have to be divided among the age categories in such a way that the age structure within the category of exchangeable jobs before and after the reorganisation remains proportionally the same. In each age category, the employee(s) with the fewest years of service will be the ones first in line for dismissal.[34] Derogation from the reflection principle is allowed to a limited extent and included in the Redundancy Regulations. In Section 16 of the Redundancy

32 Redundancy Regulations of 23 April 2015, Government Gazette (*Staatscourant*) 2015, 12685.

33 For derogation from the reflection principle, also: E. van Fenema & T. Ridder, 'Opzegging op de a- en b- grond volgens de WWZ', *ArbeidsRecht* 2014/50.

34 *Parliamentary Papers II* 2013/14, 33818, no. 3, pp. 46-47; see M.A. de Blécourt, M. Diepenbach & R. Hampsink, 'Maatwerk bij het bepalen van de ontslagvolgorde: nu en na de Wet Werk en Zekerheid', in: L.C.J. Sprengers & G.W. van der Voet (Eds.), *Arbeidsrechtelijke reflecties 2014*, Deventer: Kluwer 2014, pp. 157-209.

Regulations, an alternative is included that may be adopted in the collective labour agreement, in which a maximum of 10% of the total number of employees who are eligible for dismissal may be left out of consideration. The ground for this is above-average performance (or the expectation that there will be above-average development in the future), provided all employees are sufficiently informed and all employees are offered the same possibilities. Derogation from the reflection principle for older employees, in addition to the fact that the UWV might not give permission to terminate the employment relationship, also constitutes a tax risk. If the dismissal scheme in that case can be considered a disguised early retirement scheme, the employer will run the risk of a penalty of 52% of the dismissal compensation (Section 32ba of the Dutch Wages and Salaries Tax Act 1964 (*Wet op de loonbelasting 1964*)). The age group 55 years and older is especially susceptible as a risk group in this context. The tax authorities also impose this early retirement scheme (RVU, *Regeling voor vervroegd uittreden*) penalty on the employer in the event of voluntary resignation schemes.

1.3.2.2 Prolonged illness (b ground)

If the employee is incapacitated for work for two years, the illness will constitute a reasonable ground for termination of the employment contract. It must be plausible that the employee will not recover within twenty-six weeks or have the possibility to be placed in an adapted job within that period, and the employee – with or without the aid of training – cannot be reassigned within a reasonable period to a suitable job.[35]

1.3.2.3 UWV procedure (a and b grounds)

The Minister of Social Affairs and Employment worked out the way in which the UWV procedure is organised in the 'UWV Dismissal Procedure Regulations'.[36] A UWV form is used to submit both the application and the following defence electronically to the UWV. If the application submitted is not complete, the employer will be given the opportunity to complete it within eight days of notification to that effect by the UWV. The UWV may allow a second round of hearing from both sides.[37] Depending on the basis, the UWV may obtain expert advice on occupational options to perform work as far as health is concerned. In that case, the parties will then have the possibility to respond to this advice. The UWV will take a decision to give permission or not on the basis of all the information. If the request is based on business economic reasons, the UWV can still decide to present the request to the dismissal advisory committee for advice. This is not standard procedure.

The starting point is that an application for dismissal is in principle settled within a period of four weeks.

35 Under Section 10 of the Redundancy Regulations, a reasonable period means a period equal to the notice period; *Parliamentary Papers II* 2013/14, 33818, no. 3, p. 45. See also: E. van Fenema & T. Ridder, 'Opzegging op de a- en b-grond volgens de WWZ', *ArbeidsRecht* 2014/50.

36 See: UWV Dismissal Procedure Regulations (*Regeling UWV ontslagprocedure*) of 23 April 2015, Government Gazette 2015, 12688.

37 Section 4 UWV Dismissal Procedure Regulations.

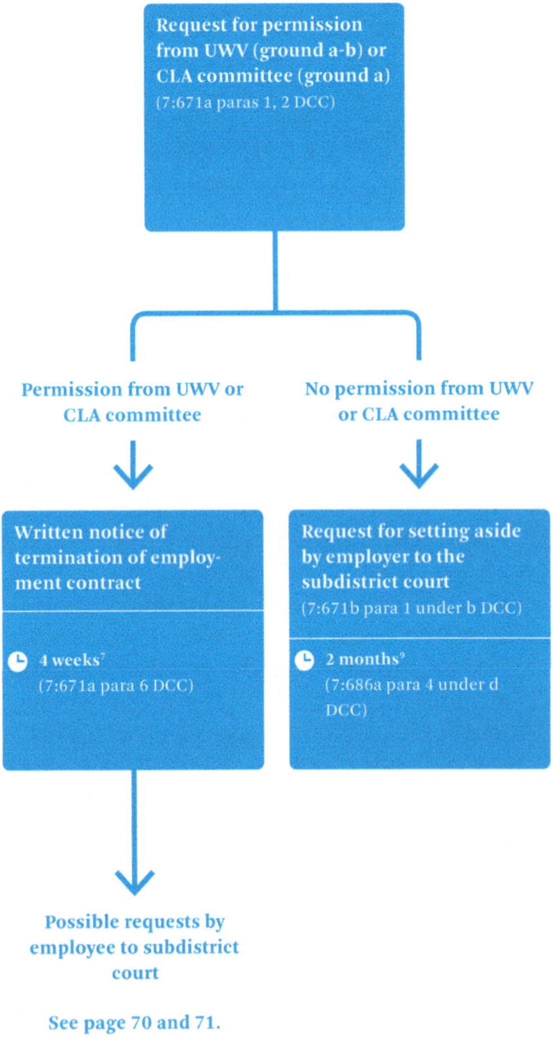
Request for permission from UWV (ground a-b) or CLA committee (ground a)
(7:671a paras 1, 2 DCC)
Permission from UWV or CLA committee
No permission from UWV or CLA committee
Written notice of termination of employment contract
4 weeks[7]
(7:671a para 6 DCC)
Request for setting aside by employer to the subdistrict court
(7:671b para 1 under b DCC)
2 months[9]
(7:686a para 4 under d DCC)
Possible requests by employee to subdistrict court
See page 70 and 71.

Practice shows that – thus far – this is too ambitious a pursuit. This is dealt with by receiving additional questions from the UWV, which means that the period of four weeks has not yet started.[38] Moreover, the computer system still has teething problems. The so-called C form that has to be completed in addition to the A and B forms contains too many small blocks in which text can be included as to why the job has been cut, for example. At the time this book was written, an additional letter still had to be used for substantiation.

The time between the date on which the complete request for permission from the UWV is received and the date on which permission is given may be deducted from the notice period. A notice period of at least one month must remain.

1.3.2.4 Term of validity of permission from the UWV

Permission from the UWV is valid for only four weeks (Book 7, Section 671a subsection 6 BW). If a request is refused, a new request to give permission can be submitted to the UWV, provided fresh facts and circumstances have become evident. This period of four weeks is most unfortunate, particularly in connection with the scheduling of larger collective dismissals.[39] In a collective dismissal, jobs are not usually all cut at the same time, but instead it is done in phases. Under the Wwz it is no longer possible to submit a so-called umbrella application for dis-

38 See: http://www.uwv.nl/werkgevers/werknemer-en-ontslag/na-ontslagaanvraag-via-uwv/.

39 Collective dismissal: an employer who intends to terminate the employment contracts of at least 20 employees, employed in one field of work, within a period of three months.

missal, under which all dismissals fall, and subsequently to receive permission from the UWV in due course. Consequently, under the Wwz it comes down to very precise scheduling for submitting individual dismissal applications. This will be difficult, especially for outsourcing or offshoring cases. Because of the longer training periods and transfers of work, the time periods required for those transitions are difficult to estimate precisely in advance. The dismissal permit could simply expire during the time that the employee was still needed. This does not seem to have been well thought out.

The short processing time at the UWV, as well as the short validity term of the permission, make it difficult to arrive at a settlement. Moreover, the employer will usually want to submit the A and B forms to the UWV first before telling the employee that his/her job will be cut and before offering the employee a termination agreement to end the employment. After all, if the employee reports sick after the A and B forms have been submitted, sickness will not form an obstacle to terminating employment after the UWV has granted permission. The UWV must receive the C form (substantiation of the dismissal), however, within eight days after receipt of the A and B forms. Furthermore, after signing the termination agreement – should it be offered – the employee will still have two weeks' reflection time. The schedule will be tight, possibly too tight. UWV has meanwhile found something that may well help, but does not remove the problem.[40] The UWV gives parties

40 For an answer to the question of whether the reflection period can be done away with by contract by including a pro forma termination in the termination agreement, see E.M. Hoogeveen, 'De opzegging met instemming, de

the possibility to request postponement of the eight-day period to submit the C form if the parties state that they want to conclude a termination agreement. If the parties reach agreement on termination by mutual consent based on a termination agreement, after 14 days the UWV will ask whether the employee has terminated the agreement. If that is the case, the employer will still have to submit the C form and the UWV procedure will continue to run.[41] This postponement by 14 days is also possible – at the request of both parties – after submission of the C form.

1.3.2.5 Notice period

Notice must be given at the end of the month, unless a different date for this has been designated in a written agreement or by custom. The notice period to be observed by the employer in the event that on the date of notice, an employment contract:

a. has lasted less than five years: one month;
b. has lasted five years or more, but less than ten years: two months;
c. has lasted ten years or more but less than fifteen years: three months; and
d. has lasted fifteen years or more: four months.

The notice period for the employer can be shortened only in a collective labour agreement (hereinafter 'CLA') or by regulations laid down by or on behalf of the competent executive body. The period can be extended in writing.

---

beëindigingsovereenkomst en de bedenktermijn: nieuwe wegen vol valkuilen', *ArbeidsRecht* 2014/48.

41 See the 'Application for a dismissal permit for business economic reasons' form, Parts A, B and C.

The notice period to be observed by the employee is one month. Derogation from the notice period for the employee is possible provided it is laid down in writing. If it is extended, it may not be for longer than six months and, for the employer, the period may not be shorter than double the time that it is for the employee.

Under Book 7, Section 672 subsection 9 BW, the party who gives notice of termination on an earlier date than the one that applies between the parties will owe the other party compensation equal to the monetary value of the salary owed for the period that the employment contract would have continued in the event of the normal notice period. In that case, termination is called defective.

1.3.2.6 Prohibitions on termination

1.3.2.6.1 'During' prohibitions on termination (Book 7, Section 670 subsections 1 to 4 and subsection 10 BW)[42]

a. The employer cannot terminate the employment contract if the employee cannot perform his/her work due to **illness**, unless the incapacity has lasted at least two years (Book 7, Section 670 subsection 1 BW). To calculate the two years, periods of incapacity as a result of pregnancy prior to maternity leave and periods of incapacity during maternity leave (Section 3:1 subsection 2 and subsection 3 of the Work and Care Act (*Wet arbeid en zorg*) are not taken into consideration. Furthermore, periods of incapacity other than those mentioned above are added up if they follow

42 A 'during' prohibition is a ban on dismissal 'during' a particular period in the employee's contract period.

each other with an interruption of less than four weeks or if they immediately precede and follow a period in which maternity leave is taken. This only differs if the incapacity cannot reasonably be considered to have arisen from the same cause. The employer **can indeed** terminate the employment contract if the incapacity started **after** a request for permission from the UWV to terminate the employment contract (Book 7, Section 671a BW) or from the committee (Book 7, Section 671a subsection 2 BW) has been received (Book 7, Section 670 subsection 1 BW). The prohibition in Book 7, Section 670 subsection 1 (a) BW, i.e. no termination during two years of illness, does not apply if the employee fails without proper grounds to comply with his/her obligations to cooperate with the reasonable instructions of an expert, to cooperate with the action plan or to perform suitable work as referred to in Book 7, Section 680a BW. The employer must first warn the employee to comply with his/her obligations and must have discontinued the salary in accordance with Book 7, Section 629 subsection 7 BW.

b. The employer cannot terminate an employee's employment contract during her **pregnancy**. To substantiate the pregnancy, the employer may require a statement by a doctor or an obstetrician. Nor can the employer terminate the employment contract during the period in which she takes maternity leave as included in Section 3:1 subsection 3 of the Work and Care Act. The employer cannot terminate the employment contract for six weeks following the maternity leave after resumption of work, or following a period of incapacity to perform work that is caused by the birth or the preceding pregnancy and that follows maternity leave (Book 7, Section 670 subsection 2 BW).

c. The employer cannot terminate an employment contract with an employee who cannot perform the stipulated work because he is in **compulsory military service** or alternative military service (Book 7, Section 670 subsection 3 BW).
d. The employer cannot terminate an employment contract with an employee who **is a member** of a **works council, central works council, group works council, standing committee of those councils, business unit committee of the works council or employee representative body.**[43]
e. The employer cannot terminate an employment contract with an employee who **is a member** of **a special negotiating group or a European works council, SE**[44] **works council, SCE**[45] **works council or who is a representative in another way responsible for providing information to and consulting with employees.**
f. The same holds for a **secretary** the employer has added to the works council or the employee representative body (Book 7, Section 670 subsection 4 BW).
g. Nor can the employer terminate an employment contract with an employee who is on a **list of candidates** for a works council or employee representative body or who was a member of a works council, central works council, group works council or a committee of those

43 As referred to in the European Works Councils Act (*Wet op de Europese ondernemingsraden* (Wet EOR)), Employee Involvement (European companies) Act (*Wet rol werknemers bij Europese rechtspersonen* (WRW-ER)).

44 SE: European Company.

45 SCE: European Cooperative Society.

councils, of an employee representative body or a special negotiating group less than two years ago. The same holds for a European works council, SE works council or SCE works council (Book 7, Section 670 subsection 10 BW).[46]

There are exceptions to the 'during' prohibitions on termination which are included in Book 7, Section 670a BW.

The 'during' prohibitions on termination are not applicable if the employee agrees to termination in writing, termination (with immediate effect) during the probationary period, or if it concerns termination with immediate effect for an urgent cause that was communicated to the employee immediately. Nor are the 'during' prohibitions applicable if the ground for termination of the employment contract is a business shutdown – closure of the company (a ground) or if a dismissal at state pension age or retirement age is concerned (Book 7, Section 670a subsection 2). There are additional special rules if termination is based on an a ground other than due to discontinuation of the company's operations, and the employee was employed for at least 26 weeks in the job to be cut (Book 7, Section 670a subsection 3). In that case the prohibition in Book 7, Section 670 subsection 2 BW does not apply (termination during pregnancy) if the activities in the division of the company where the employee works are exclusively or primarily discontinued. This does not apply if the employee has taken maternity leave as referred to in Section 3:1 of the Dutch Work and Care

46 As referred to in the European Works Councils Act (Wet EOR), Employee Involvement (European companies) Act (WRW-ER).

Act. The prohibition in Book 7, Section 670 subsection 3 BW (termination during compulsory military service) does not apply either if the activities in the division of the company where the employee works are exclusively or primarily discontinued. Lastly, the prohibitions in Book 7, Section 670 subsection 4 (member of the works council and the councils mentioned by name) and subsection 10 BW (list of candidates) do not apply.

Although the abovementioned exceptions provide some points of reference for dismissing sick employees as well dismissing staff during a reorganisation, they are very limited. After all, closure of the whole company has to be involved.[47]

1.3.2.6.2 'Due to' prohibitions on termination (Book 7, Section 670 subsection 5 to 9 inclusive BW)

The employer cannot terminate the employment contract due to:

a. **Membership of a trade union** (Book 7, Section 670 subsection 5 BW).
b. **Attending meetings** as referred to in Book 7, Section 643 BW, provided he/she has leave to do so (Book 7, Section 670 subsection 6 BW).
c. A right to **adoption leave** or leave to take in a foster child as referred to in Section 3:2 of the Dutch Work and Care Act, taking short- and **long-term care leave** as referred to in Section 5 of the Wwz, or the employee's right to parental leave as referred to in Section 6 of the Dutch Work and Care Act (Book 7, Section 670 subsection 7 BW).

47 See *Parliamentary Papers II* 2013/14, 33818, no. 3, pp. 102-103.

d. **Transfer of an company** as referred to in Book 7, Section 662 subsection 2(a) BW (Book 7, Section 670 subsection 8 BW).
e. Not agreeing to **working on Sundays** (Book 7, Section 670 subsection 9 BW).

The employer cannot terminate an employment contract in conflict with equal treatment legislation pursuant to Book 7, Section 646 BW (discriminating between men and women), Book 7, Section 648 BW (discrimination in working conditions based on the number of working hours) or Book 7, Section 649 BW (discrimination in working conditions based on the temporary nature of the employment contract) or any other prohibition on discrimination. This is also called the prohibitions on discrimination. There are no exceptions to the 'due to' prohibitions on termination.[48]

1.3.3 Setting aside of the employment contract by the sub-district court (Book 7, Section 671b subsection 1 BW)

If the employer wants to terminate an employment contract on a so-called c to h ground and does not choose the consent route or the termination agreement, or if the employee is unwilling to cooperate in this, it must submit an application to the sub-district court to set aside the employment contract (Book 7, Section 671b subsection 1 BW).

48 *Parliamentary Papers II* 2013/14, 33818, no. 3, p. 32.

These grounds are:

a. **Incapacity on a regular basis to perform the stipulated work** as a result of the employee's **illness** or disability with unacceptable consequences for the business operations (**c ground**). Incapacity to perform the stipulated work can not be due to the employer taking insufficient care of the employee's working conditions. If the employer wants to put this ground forward in order to terminate the employment, it must submit a statement from an expert that the employee has often been absent due to illness (Book 7, Section 671b in conjunction with Book 7, Section 629a BW). Moreover, the employer must be able to demonstrate that this absence has unacceptable consequences for its business operations. The employer must submit a statement by an expert from the UWV. The employer must make it plausible as well that the employee will not recover within 26 weeks, i.e. a considerable improvement of the situation, or that the stipulated work cannot be performed in an adapted form. The employer will also have to demonstrate that reassignment to another suitable job, with or without the aid of training, will not be among the possibilities within a reasonable time.
b. **Incapacity** on the part of the employee to **perform the stipulated work,** other than as a result of the employee's sickness or disability (**d ground**). This ground concerns the employee not performing adequately and he/she not meeting the job requirements due to inability or incompetence. The employer must be able to demonstrate that it has done enough and offered the employee sufficient possibilities to improve the employee's performance. This can be done, for

example, on the basis of a Performance Improvement Plan ('PIP'), which not only includes the points on which the employee needs to improve his/her performance, but also includes specific actions to be taken by the employee to improve his/her performance. The document may also include what the employer will undertake to help the employee to improve his/her performance. Timelines also need to be agreed that make clear the time limit for improvements clear to the employee. If the non-performance is clearly the result of the employer not paying sufficient attention to training, there will be no reasonable ground for dismissal.[49] The employer will have to demonstrate as well that there are no possibilities within a reasonable period for reassigning the employee to another suitable job, with or without the aid of training. Section 10 subsection 1 of the Redundancy Regulations stipulates that the reasonable period is the notice period applicable to that employee.[50]

c. **Imputable acts or omissions** on the part of the employee (**e ground**). The requirements set for an employee must be those used in general practice and not excessive.[51] It should be clear to the employee what is not acceptable at his/her employer's company and the employee must be warned in most cases. Companies usually have a code of conduct showing what is

49 *Parliamentary Papers II* 2013/14, 33818, no. 3, p. 44.

50 See also: S.F. Sagel, 'Werk en zekerheid: ontslagrecht doen in tijden van hard en fast rules', (Inaugural lecture of 5 September 2014, Leiden University); A.J. Swelheim, 'Draait de redelijke grond de ontbindingsprocedure op slot?', *ArbeidsRecht* 2014/51.

51 *Parliamentary Papers II* 2013/14, 33818, no. 3, p. 45.

considered unacceptable. It has emerged from recent a case law ruling by the Sub-District Court of Rotterdam that calling a co-worker a Nazi does not qualify as an urgent cause if it is not sufficiently evident that it had been expressly pointed out to the employee that such statements would not be tolerated and could result in summary dismissal.[52]

It is important for the employer to observe the code of conduct, in any case concerning acts or omissions. Another example is regularly arriving late. The circumstances of the case are important and will also be taken into consideration. For instance, there may be mitigating circumstances for the employee as a result of which the act or omission is not imputable. This e ground can also be based on non-performance by the employee, provided he/she can be blamed for this. The initial rulings of sub-district courts show that sub-district court set store by reports of interviews and assessment reports in which the non-performance is recorded. The employee must be given the opportunity to improve his/her performance (for example, through coaching).[53] The e ground also covers failure of a sick employee to comply with statutory requirements in relation to his/her re-integration obligations, provided he/she has been cautioned to do so and the employer has discontinued the salary for this reason. With this ground, the employer is not required

52 Sub-District Court of Rotterdam 16 October 2015, ECLI:NL:RBROT:2015:7563, *AR* 2015/1038.

53 Overijssel District Court 16 October 2015, ECLI:NL:RBOVE:2015:4663, *AR* 2015/1004; District Court of The Hague 21 September 2015, ECLI:NL:RB:DHA:2015:11165, *AR* 2015/0949.

to examine reassignment possibilities.[54] (The term 'urgent cause' in Book 7, Section 677 subsection 1 BW and the e ground can overlap. Examples include theft, fraud or insulting or being violent towards a co-worker. Immediacy, however, is not required for the e ground.[55] Moreover, no culpability is required for an urgent cause.)

d. Refusal by the employee to perform the stipulated work due to **serious conscientious objections (f ground)**. The employer must demonstrate that the employee has an insurmountable objection to performing the stipulated work on the basis of religious, generally accepted ethnic or political grounds. Examples of this may include having to insure fur coats or work on the construction of a nuclear power plant. The employer must also make it plausible that the work cannot be performed in an adapted form.[56] Work in an adapted form means without performing tasks that lead to actions against which a conscientious objection exists. The employer will have to demonstrate that reassignment to another suitable job, with or without the aid of training, is not among the possibilities.
e. A **disrupted employment relationship (g ground)**. The employment relationship must be disrupted to the extent that the employer cannot reasonably be required to allow the employment contract to continue. The disruption must be serious and long lasting. It is also possible to terminate the employment contract due to a less long-lasting disruption if it is serious

54 *Parliamentary Papers II* 2013/14, 33818, no. 3, p. 45.
55 See *Parliamentary Papers II* 2013/14, 33818, no. 3, p. 120.
56 *Parliamentary Papers II* 2013/14, 33818, no. 7, p. 131.

to the extent that the employer cannot reasonably be required to continue the employment contract.[57] The initial rulings show that sub-district courts are not easily persuaded that there is a disrupted employment relationship.[58] In most cases, sub-district courts rule that a mediation process should be gone through first before it can be established that there actually is a disrupted employment relationship. Furthermore, the North Netherlands District Court in Assen held that it is up to the employer to resolve underlying points of contention between employees, with or without the aid of external coaching.[59]

f. **Circumstances other** than those mentioned above, which are of such a nature that the employer cannot reasonably be required to allow the employment contract to continue (**h ground**). This ground is explicitly not intended as an open residual category. Only special cases that do not have their origins in a to g grounds can fall under this. Legislative history mentions detention, illegality of the employee and the employer not having a work permit.[60] Examples are also given in the legislative history of a football trainer who was dismissed because of poor match results or a manager with whom a difference of opinion exists on the policy to be pursued, if there is no question of non-performance, or at any rate if that cannot be the

57 *Parliamentary Papers II* 2013/14, 33818, no. 3, p. 46.

58 District Court of Amsterdam 6 October 2015, ECLI:NL: RBAMS:2015:7278, *AR* 2015/1028.

59 District Court of North Netherlands 24 september 2014, ECLI: RBNNE:2015:4508, *AR* 2015/0912.

60 *Parliamentary Papers II* 2013/14, 33818, no. 3, pp. 46 and 99.

Request for setting aside by employer to the subdistrict court (ground c-h, or a-b if permission by UWV or CLA committee has been refused)
(7:671b para 1 DCC)

Granting of request for setting aside and any counter application made by the employee for the award of fair compensation if the setting aside is the consequence of seriously culpable acts or omissions by the employer and/or transition compensation
(7:671b para 8 under c in conjunction with 7:673 DCC)

Possible requests by employee to subdistrict court
See page 73.

Refusal of setting aside

appeal

ground for dismissal.[61] The employer examining reassignment does not play a part in this ground.[62]

1.3.4 Setting aside by the sub-district court on the a ground or b ground

In some cases the court with the power to terminate the employment contract also has jurisdiction over a or b grounds. This is the case first of all if the UWV has refused to give permission for termination on the a or b ground. In that case the employer can ask the sub-district court to set aside the employment contract on these grounds, as follows from Book 7, Section 671b subsection 1(b) BW. The sub-district court also has jurisdiction to set aside on the a or b ground if there is a fixed-term contract that cannot be terminated early (Book 7, Section 671b subsection 1(c) BW) (see Section 1.5 regarding termination of a fixed-term contract without an early termination option).

1.3.5 Review of the application to set aside and prohibitions on termination

The sub-district court can allow the application to set aside the employment contract if the conditions for its referred to in Book 7, Section 669 BW are met. Moreover, pursuant to the second subsection of Book 7, Section 671b BW, no prohibition on termination may be applicable.

Setting aside of employment contracts by the sub-district court is nevertheless possible in the event of a

61 *Parliamentary Papers II* 2013/14, 33818, no. 7, p. 130.
62 See also: A.J. Swelheim, 'Draait de redelijke grond de ontbindingsprocedure op slot?', *ArbeidsRecht* 2014/51.

'during' prohibition on termination in a number of cases mentioned in the Act.

First of all, the prohibition on termination during illness does not apply if the sickness started after the sub-district court received the application for setting aside (Book 7, Section 671b subsection 7 BW).

The sub-district court can also set aside the employment contract even if a 'during' prohibition on termination applies if the application to set aside the employment contract does not concern circumstances that would give rise to the prohibitions on termination; or if the circumstances are such that the employment contract should end in the interests of the employee (Book 7, Section 671b subsection 6 BW). This does not apply if the request for setting aside is based on an a ground (after the UWV has refused permission for termination or for early termination of a fixed-term employment contract without an early termination option). This is a considerable limitation and in our view unworkable for companies. Under the old law, sick employees – who had been sick for less than two years – could be dismissed in the event of a reorganisation provided the dismissal was not related to the sickness. This could not be done via the UWV but employers had the option of requesting the sub-district court to set aside the employment contract. This is no longer possible under the current law.[63] A sick employee can only be dismissed if the company closes completely (Book 7, Section 670a subsection 2(d) BW). Because these rules are so restrictive, employers will prefer to go to the UWV to request permission to terminate the employment contract on the

63 R.S. van Coevorden, 'Bijzondere opzegverboden', *Tijdschrift voor Arbeidsrechtpraktijk* 2014/1, p. 47.

basis of an a ground (business economic reasons). They will do so in any case before presenting a termination agreement to the employee, and probably even before the employee hears that his/her job will be cut, in order to prevent employees from reporting sick before the employer has submitted the application to the UWV. This side effect is undesirable for the employer and almost inhumane for the employee.

1.3.6 Time at which the employment contract is set aside

Under Book 7, Section 671b subsection 8 BW, the sub-district court that sets aside the employment contract is not at liberty to determine the date on which the employment contract is set aside. The sub-district court must set aside the employment contract on the date on which the employment contract would have ended normally, with deduction of the time taken by the proceedings. At least one month must remain. If the employment contract is set aside owing to serious imputable acts or omissions on the part of the employee, the sub-district court can bring the termination date forward.

1.3.7 Fair compensation

If the sub-district court allows the request for setting aside, it can award the employee fair compensation, but only if the employment contract has been set aside as a result of serious imputable acts or omissions on the part of the employer (Book 7, Section 671b subsection 8(c) BW). (See more about this in Section 3.2.)

1.4 Dismissal during a special situation or of a special person

In certain special situations or for special persons, the employer must observe exceptions to the normal dismissal rules, as discussed above. These special situations and the persons classified as 'special' most often, as well as the exceptions to the normal dismissal rules, will be dealt with below.

1.4.1 Dismissal during the probationary period (Book 7, Section 671 subsection 1(b) in conjunction with Book 7, Section 676 BW)

The requirement of agreement does not apply to dismissal during the probationary period and no reasonable ground is required (Book 7, Section 671 subsection 1(b) and Book 7, Section 669 subsection 7 BW). The 'during' prohibitions on termination do not apply either (Book 7, Section 670a subsection 2(b) BW). The 'due to' prohibitions on termination remain fully in effect. This means that dismissing an employee in the probationary period due to illness is not allowed.[64] The employment contract can also be terminated during the probationary period without a notice period (Book 7, Section 676 BW). The probationary period clause must, however, be legally valid. In an indefinite employment contract, a two-month probationary period is the maximum that can be agreed (Book 7, Section 652 subsection 3 BW). Employment contracts of

64 P.L.M. Schneider, 'Het loondoorbetalingsbeding, het proeftijdbeding en het concurrentiebeding in de Wet werk en zekerheid', *Tijdschrift voor Arbeidsrechtpraktijk* 2014/1, p. 14.

up to six months may not include a probationary period (Book 7, Section 652 subsection 4 BW). Employment contracts from six months to two years may include a probationary period of one month; for those entered into for two years or more, the probationary period is two months (Book 7, Section 652 subsection 5 BW).

1.4.2 Summary dismissal (Book 7, Section 671 subsection 1(c) in conjunction with Book 7, Section 677 subsection 1 BW)

For valid summary dismissal, there must be an **'urgent cause'** that justifies immediate termination of the employment contract. Termination must take place immediately. In this context, immediately means that, on suspecting an urgent cause, the employer is given a short time to investigate the facts, gather evidence and obtain legal advice on the question of whether the facts discovered justify an urgent cause for summary dismissal. After dismissal, the employee must be informed immediately and sufficiently clearly of the termination. A very short time span is allowed between termination and notification of dismissal.[65] Book 7, Section 678 subsection 2 BW contains a non-limitative list of situations in which urgent cause can be considered to exist for the employer. According to the law, the following cases inter alia constitute urgent cause:

a. When concluding the employment contract, the employee misled the employer by showing forged or falsified references, or intentionally gave false information about the way in which his/her last

65 *Parliamentary Papers II* 2013/14, 33818, no. 3, p. 115.

employment contract was changed. Concealing an ailment constitutes an urgent cause if the employee should have known that he/she was not suitable for the job because of the ailment. An employee is entitled to remain silent on matters about which an employer may not ask, such as pregnancy.

b. The employee proves to be seriously lacking in competency or is not suitable for the job for which he/she was contracted.
c. The employee is drunk or disorderly despite warnings to desist from this behaviour.
d. The employee commits theft, embezzlement, fraud or other serious offences thus proving him- or herself to be unworthy of the employer's trust.
e. The employee commits assault, insults or seriously threatens the employer, his family members or household members or co-employees.
f. The employee incites the employer, his family members or household members, or his co-employees, or attempts to incite them, to perform acts contrary to the laws or good morals.
g. The employee, intentionally or, despite warning, recklessly, damages or exposes the employer's property of to serious danger.
h. The employee, intentionally or, despite warning, recklessly, exposes himself or others to serious danger.
i. The employee discloses particulars regarding the household or business of the employer that he/she should keep secret.
j. The employee stubbornly refuses to comply with reasonable orders or assignments given to him/her by or on behalf of the employer. In this context, the employer must take any convincing objections

that the employee may have into account. Even if the employee refuses for the first time to perform a reasonable assignment, such can justify summary dismissal, depending on the circumstances. Urgent cause in the case of sickness will not easily stand up to scrutiny. If the employer were able to assume on the basis of advice from the occupational physician that the employee was able to work, summary dismissal is not justified if the employee nonetheless proves to be incapacitated for work.

k. The employee otherwise grossly disregards his/her duties under the employment contract.
l. The employee is or remains unable to perform the stipulated work due to intention or recklessness.

In assessing summary dismissal, the court must assess the circumstances of the case in their interrelationship and coherence. The court must weigh the nature and gravity of the urgent cause against the personal circumstances put forward by the employee. Summary dismissal may be valid if the employee is not to blame. Behaviour outside working hours can constitute urgent cause.[66] The nature of the urgent cause can obviate the need for blame. Not only must a summary dismissal be so serious with respect to cause that it justifies dismissal without a preventive review, it must also be effected immediately and communicated immediately to the employee. In practice, this is the reason why, together with – as Van der Kind calls it – the possibility of a jumble of proceedings, the advice is

66 See also G.J.J. Heerma van Voss and J.M. van Slooten, *NJB* (Netherlands Law Journal) 2008, p. 971.

generally not to choose the route of summary dismissal.[67] This gives rise to the question of whether it is possible to offer the employee a termination proposal prior to summary dismissal. Under previous legislation, an employee was usually suspended, with mention of the urgent cause, and told that the intention was to dismiss him/her with an offer of a termination agreement. The employee was allowed to think about it for a few days. If he/she chose not to sign the termination agreement, he/she was dismissed on the spot. Under the Wwz, the reflection period is 14 days. Can the employee still be legally dismissed summarily after those 14 days? Time will tell. It is argued in the literature that this is still be possible because the passing of the time due to the statutory reflection period is not due to the employer's failure to act expeditiously.[68]

If the urgent cause is indeed urgent, termination is immediate and communicated to the employee simultaneously, then no consent is needed from the employee, nor is a preventive review of the dismissal by the UWV or the sub-district court necessary (Book 7, Section 671 subsection 1(c) BW). Moreover, in that case the 'during' prohibitions on termination do not apply (Book 7, Section 670a subsection 2(c) BW) and the employer does not have to pay compensation for not observing the notice period. If the summary dismissal is the result of serious imputable acts or omissions on the part of the employee, the employee will not be entitled either to transition compensation (Book 7, Section 673 subsection 7(c) BW). A valid summary

67 For a survey on summary dismissal under the Wwz, see O. Van der Kind, 'Ontslag op staande voet onder de WWZ', *ArbeidsRecht* 2014/59.

68 S.F. Sagel, 'Het ontslag op staande voet en de WWZ', *Tijdschrift Recht en Arbeid* 2015/45.

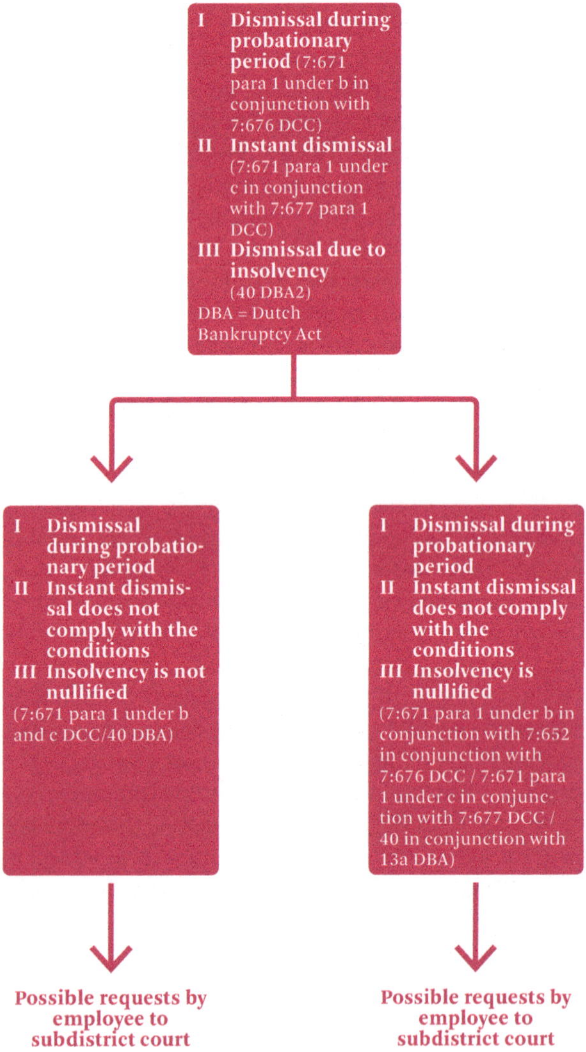
I Dismissal during probationary period (7:671 para 1 under b in conjunction with 7:676 DCC)
II Instant dismissal (7:671 para 1 under c in conjunction with 7:677 para 1 DCC)
III Dismissal due to insolvency (40 DBA2)
DBA = Dutch Bankruptcy Act
I Dismissal during probationary period
II Instant dismissal does not comply with the conditions
III Insolvency is not nullified
(7:671 para 1 under b and c DCC/40 DBA)
I Dismissal during probationary period
II Instant dismissal does not comply with the conditions
III Insolvency is nullified
(7:671 para 1 under b in conjunction with 7:652 in conjunction with 7:676 DCC / 7:671 para 1 under c in conjunction with 7:677 DCC / 40 in conjunction with 13a DBA)
Possible requests by employee to subdistrict court
Possible requests by employee to subdistrict court

dismissal does not always mean that the employee has committed imputable acts. That is why it is possible that employers who dismiss employees summarily and legally still have to pay transition compensation because the employee did not commit any serious imputable acts or omissions.

1.4.3 Dismissal of a director or officer (Book 7, Section 671 subsection 1(e) BW)

The termination concerns **a director or officer** (director or officer under the articles of association) of a legal entity, other than a foundation or similar foreign legal entity. The director or officer who is lawfully appointed by the shareholders or the supervisory board (in most cases he/she is also registered as a director or officer in the Commercial Register of the Chamber of Commerce) has a status that is distinct from those of 'ordinary' employees. He/she has both a corporate and an employment relationship with the legal entity. The termination of his/her corporate relationship also applies as a termination of his/her employment contract, unless a prohibition on termination applies or the parties have agreed otherwise.[69] For dismissal under employment law, no consent is needed from the director or officer, nor is there a preventive review by the UWV or the sub-district court (Book 7, Section 671 subsection 1(e) BW). Book 7, Section 669 BW does not make any exception for a director or officer under the articles of association. There must be a reasonable

69 Netherlands Supreme Court (HR) 15 April 2005, *JAR* 2005/117 and HR 15 April 2005, *JAR* 2005/153.

ground for his/her dismissal.[70] If there is no reasonable ground, the director or officer under the articles of association can then request the sub-district court to award fair compensation (Book 7, Section 682 subsection 3 BW). The director or officer under the articles of association, unlike the titular director or officer, cannot, however, request reinstatement of employment under Book 2, Section 134 BW and Book 2, Section 244 BW. For legally valid termination of the corporate relationship, the director or officer under the articles of association needs to be called lawfully – in accordance with the articles of association – to (usually) a shareholders' meeting. His/her intended dismissal must be on the agenda. If the director or officer reports sick after he has received the call to the shareholders' meeting, the prohibition on termination in connection with sickness will not apply. The director or officer needs to be heard during the shareholders' meeting (Book 2, Section 8 BW) and he/she should be given the opportunity to express an advisory opinion (Book 2, Section 227 subsection 4 BW). The dismissal resolution must be validly passed, otherwise the director or officer may request to have the dismissal resolution declared null and void or nullified (Book 2, Sections 14 and 15 BW).

70 *Parliamentary Papers II* 2013/14, 33818, no. 3, pp. 27-28.

1.4.4 Dismissal on reaching the state pension age/retirement age (Book 7, Section 671 subsection 1(g) in conjunction with Book 7, Section 669 subsection 4 BW)

The employer can terminate the employment contract without a reasonable ground **on or after the date on which the employee reaches the age of entitlement to state pension or the retirement age applicable to him/her** (Book 7, Section 669 subsection 4 BW).[71] The idea is that the

71 Since 2013 the age of entitlement to state pension has risen step-by-step from 65 years and will be 67 years in 2021. From 2022 the state pension age will rise together with the life expectancy in the Netherlands. What is meant by a different retirement age will follow from a new legislative proposal, Social Security (Miscellaneous Provisions) Act 2016

reasonable ground lies in reaching the age of entitlement to state pension or a different retirement age. No transition compensation is due either (Book 7, Section 673 subsection 7(b) BW). The applicable notice period does, however, have to be observed (from 1 January 2016, one month if state pension age has been reached).[72] In order to use reaching state pension or a different retirement age as the ground to terminate the employment contract, however, the employment contract must have been entered into before this state pension or other retirement age was reached.

Note that termination at an age younger than the state pension age is usually in conflict with the Dutch Equal Treatment in Employment (Age Discrimination) Act (*Wet gelijke behandeling op grond van leeftijd bij de arbeid* (WGBL)) and is not allowed. Opinions are divided on whether a random termination at an age after the state pension age would also be in conflict with the WGBL.[73] Case law will have to decide this.

It could be that the employer and employee have included in the employment contract or collective labour agreement that the employment contract will end by operation of law on reaching the age of entitlement to state pension, a so-called retirement dismissal clause.

(*Verzamelwet SZW 2016*): this is the dismissal age referred to in a pension dismissal clause, *Parliamentary Papers II* 2014/15, 34273, no. 3.

72 A temporary exception has been made for incapacitated persons entitled to state pension.

73 See B. Degelink, 'Het pensioenontslag onder de WWZ: nuttig of inflexibel?', *ArbeidsRecht* 2015/47; J.W. Boelhouwer, 'De pensioengerechtigde leeftijd in de WWZ', *ArbeidsRecht* 2015/25.

In that case the employment contract will indeed end by operation of law without a reasonable a to g ground being required, a notice period having to be observed or transition compensation being due. If a retirement dismissal clause has been agreed but the employee continues to work after reaching state pension age, a new employment relationship will start.

Employer who has reached State pension or different retirement age[10]
(7:671 para 1 under g in conjunction with 7:669 para 4 DCC)

↓

Possible requests by employee to subdistrict court

See page 62.

1.5 Termination of a fixed-term employment contract without an early termination clause

In principle, a fixed-term employment contract ends when the term of the employment contract expires and the employer has decided not to offer the employee an extension or a new employment contract. In that case, the fixed-term employment contract will end by operation of law (Book 7, Section 667 subsection 1 BW).

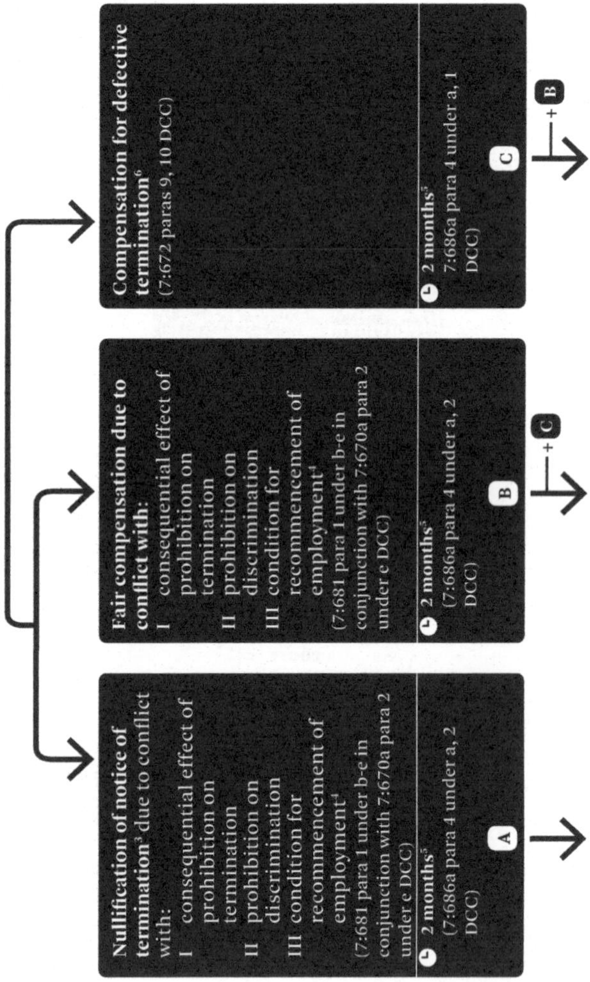
Nullification of notice of termination[3] due to conflict with:
I consequential effect of prohibition on termination
II prohibition on discrimination
III condition for recommencement of employment[4]
(7:681 para 1 under b-e in conjunction with 7:670a para 2 under e DCC)
2 months[5]
(7:686a para 4 under a, 2 DCC)
A
appeal
Fair compensation due to conflict with:
I consequential effect of prohibition on termination
II prohibition on discrimination
III condition for recommencement of employment[4]
(7:681 para 1 under b-e in conjunction with 7:670a para 2 under e DCC)
2 months[5]
(7:686a para 4 under a, 2 DCC)
B
+ C
appeal
Compensation for defective termination[6]
(7:672 paras 9, 10 DCC)
2 months[5]
7:686a para 4 under a, 1 DCC)
C
+ B
appeal

Note that if there is a series of fixed-term employment contracts, the last employment contract will convert automatically into an indefinite employment contract if:

a. the series of employment contracts exceeds a period of 24 months; or
b. there are more than three successive fixed-term employment contracts.

This rule is called the 'chain rule' (because there is a 'chain' of contracts) and it can be interrupted if there is a gap of more than six months between the last and the next employment contract. The chain rule in the abovementioned variant entered into effect on 1 July 2015.[74] Previously a period of 36 months applied, with an interruption of 3 months. The chain rule also applies mutatis mutandis to consecutive employment contracts between an employee and different employers which,

74 Note: transitional law applies to the Chain Rule Section XXIIe Transitional Law (*Overgangsrecht*) stipulates that if no CLA is applicable on 30 June, the (new) chain rule will apply only to subsequent employment contracts entered into from 1 July 2015 and no more than six months after the previous employment contract. If the chain has not yet exceeded 24 months on 1 July 2015, but will indeed do so during the term of the employment contract still in effect on that date, the employment contract will still end by operation of law and not automatically be converted into an indefinite employment contract. If a CLA is indeed effect on 30 June 2015 (in which the statutory chain rule has been declared applicable or has been derogated from), the operation of the (new) chain rule will be postponed until the time that the term of the CLA expires, or until 1 July 2016 at the latest. The interruption period of more than 6 will immediately apply to intervals in effect on 1 July 2015.

with respect to the work performed, should be considered to be a successor.

1.5.1.a 'Obligation to give notice'

Under the Wwz, the employer also has the obligation to inform the employee in writing no later than one month before the fixed-term employment contract ends by operation of law (**i**) about whether or not the employment contract will be continued; and (**ii**) if the contract is to be renewed, about the conditions under which the employer wants to continue the employment contract. This is called the 'obligation to give notice' (effective 1 January 2015). The obligation to give notice does not apply to temporary employment contracts that end at a time not set on a calendar date and to employment contracts is entered into for a period of less than six months.

1.5.2 Early termination of a fixed-term employment contract

For fixed-term employment contracts without an early termination clause that need to be terminated early on an **a ground** (redundancies due to discontinuation of the company's operations or business economic circumstances) or **b ground** (due to prolonged illness or disability), an application has to be sent to the sub-district court (Book 7, Section 671b subsection 1(c) BW, see Section 1.3.4).[75]

75 See also: *Parliamentary Papers II* 2013/14, 33818, no. 3, p. 107; and see also: E. van Fenema and T. Ridder, 'Opzegging op de a- en b-grond volgens de WWZ', *ArbeidsRecht* 2014/50.

1.5.2.a Time at which the fixed-term employment contract is set aside

For fixed-term employment contracts **without** an early termination clause that the sub-district court sets aside pursuant to Book 7, Section 671b subsection 9 BW, the sub-district court has the discretionary power to set the date on which it will be set aside.[76]

1.5.2.b Compensation

If the sub-district court sets aside a fixed-term employment contract that cannot be terminated early, the court may award the employee compensation not exceeding the monetary value of the salary determined for the period that the employment contract would have lasted if it had ended by operation of law (Book 7, Section 671b subsection 9(a) BW). The employee may also be awarded fair compensation if the setting aside is the result of serious imputable acts or omissions on the part of the employer (subsection 9(b) BW) (see more about this in Section 3.2). Conversely, if setting aside is the result of serious imputable acts or omissions on the part of the employee, the employer will be awarded compensation not exceeding an amount equal to the monetary value of the salary for the period that the employment contract would have lasted if it had ended by operation of law (subsection 9(c) BW).

76 See also: D.J. Rutgers en M.C. van der Kamp, 'Naar een nieuw ontslagrecht (4): beëindigingsovereenkomst, opzeggings- en ontbindingsprocedure', *Bedrijfsjuridische Berichten* 2014/37.

Chapter 2
Consequences of violating the rules for termination of an employment contract

2.1 Possible applications by the employee after termination

Book 7, Sections 681, 682 and 672 subsection 9 BW lay down what the sanctions are if the employer acts infringes the rules for termination of an employment contract. It is doubtful whether these rules also apply to termination with the employee's consent. It could be argued that the employee's consent pertains only to avoiding the preventive review of dismissal.[77] In that case, Book 7, Sections 681 and 672 subsection 9 BW also apply to termination with consent. They do not apply if the employment contract has been ended lawfully by a termination agreement.

2.1.1 Nullification of termination

Book 7, Section 681 subsection 1(b-e) BW lays down the circumstance under which the employee can apply for

77 W.H.A.C.M. Bouwens & R.A.A. Duk, *Van der Grinten Arbeidsovereenkomstenrecht*, Deventer: Kluwer 2015, p. 370.

nullification of termination after his/her employment contract has been terminated, or for which he/she can apply for fair compensation instead. They are as follows:

a. The employer has given notice of termination without the required agreement on the part of the employee.
b. The employer has given notice of termination contrary to a special prohibition on termination (see Section 1.3.2.6.1).
c. The employer has given notice of termination contrary to a prohibition on discrimination.
d. The employer engages someone else within 26 weeks after termination on an a ground and has this other person perform the same work as the former employee without having given the former employee the opportunity to resume his/her work (i.e. a breach of the condition for recommencement of employment).

If the termination is nullified, the employment contract is deemed never to have been interrupted.

The employee must submit an application to the court within two months of the date on which the employment contract was terminated (Book 7, 686a subsection 4(a)(2) BW).

2.1.2 Reinstatement of the employment contract

Book 7, Section 682 BW lays down the circumstances under which the employee can apply for reinstatement of his/her employment contract after termination or can apply for fair compensation instead.

The employee can apply for reinstatement of the employment contract if the employment contract was terminated with permission from the UWV and such termination is in conflict with an a or b ground. If the sub-district court allows the application, the employer is obliged to offer the employee the same employment contract as before termination. Instead of reinstatement, the employee can also apply for fair compensation, but this can only be awarded if reinstatement is not reasonably possible owing to serious imputable acts or omissions on the part of the employer (see more about fair compensation in Section 3.2).

Book 7, Section 682 BW also lays down a number of rules for the termination of 'special persons'. For example, a director or officer under the articles of association can apply for fair compensation if his/her termination is contrary to Book 7, Section 669 BW or is the result of serious imputable acts or omissions on the part of the employer (subsection 3).

This cannot be claimed if termination took place with the employee's consent, nor if the dismissal took place during the probationary period or on the spot. Nor can a director or officer under the articles of association of a legal entity other than a foundation claim reinstatement of his/her employment contract. The same holds for an employee whose contract was terminated due to having reached the state pension or different retirement age.

The application must be submitted to the court within 2 months after the date on which the employment contract was terminated (Book 7, Section 686a subsection 4(a)(2) BW).

2.1.3 Defective termination

If the employer has not observed the notice period, the employee can **apply for compensation due to defective**

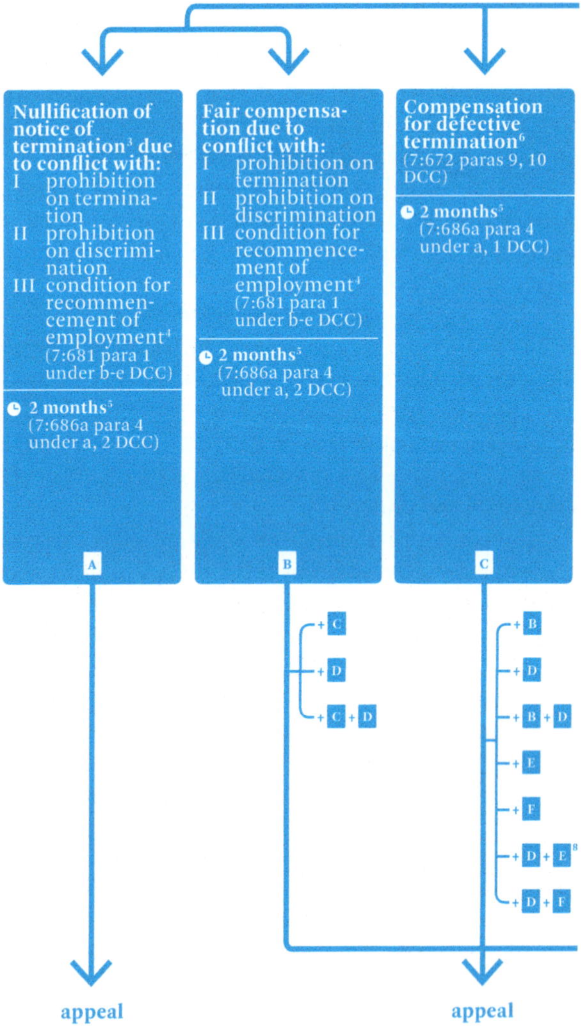
Nullification of notice of termination[3] due to conflict with:
I prohibition on termination
II prohibition on discrimination
III condition for recommencement of employment[4] (7:681 para 1 under b-e DCC)
2 months[5] (7:686a para 4 under a, 2 DCC)
A
Fair compensation due to conflict with:
I prohibition on termination
II prohibition on discrimination
III condition for recommencement of employment[4] (7:681 para 1 under b-e DCC)
2 months[5] (7:686a para 4 under a, 2 DCC)
B
+ C
+ D
+ C + D
Compensation for defective termination[6] (7:672 paras 9, 10 DCC)
2 months[5] (7:686a para 4 under a, 1 DCC)
C
+ B
+ D
+ B + D
+ E
+ F
+ D + E[8]
+ D + F
appeal
appeal

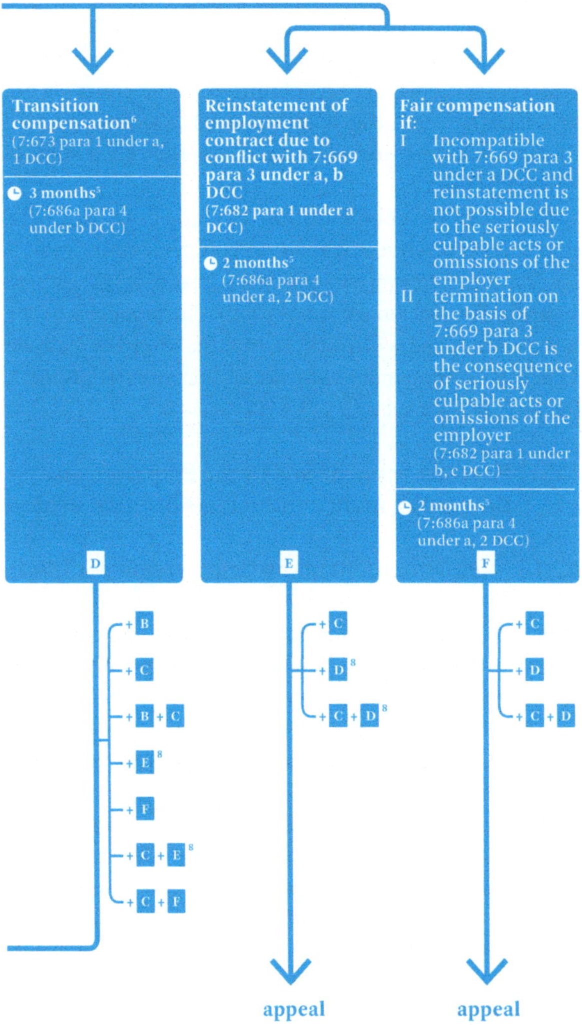
Transition compensation[6]
(7:673 para 1 under a, 1 DCC)
3 months[5]
(7:686a para 4 under b DCC)
D
+ B
+ C
+ B + C
+ E[8]
+ F
+ C + E[8]
+ C + F
Reinstatement of employment contract due to conflict with 7:669 para 3 under a, b DCC
(7:682 para 1 under a DCC)
2 months[5]
(7:686a para 4 under a, 2 DCC)
E
+ C
+ D[8]
+ C + D[8]
appeal
Fair compensation if:
I Incompatible with 7:669 para 3 under a DCC and reinstatement is not possible due to the seriously culpable acts or omissions of the employer
II termination on the basis of 7:669 para 3 under b DCC is the consequence of seriously culpable acts or omissions of the employer
(7:682 para 1 under b, c DCC)
2 months[5]
(7:686a para 4 under a, 2 DCC)
F
+ C
+ D
+ C + D
appeal

termination of his/her employment contract under Book 7, Section 672 subsection 9 and subsection 10 BW. This application must be submitted to the court within two months after the date on which the employment contract was terminated (Book 7, Section 686a subsection 4(a)(1) BW).

If transition compensation has not been paid, the employee can request transition compensation (Book 7, Section 673 subsection 1(a) BW) (see also Chapter 3 regarding transition compensation). The request must be submitted to the within three months after the date on which the employment contract was terminated (Book 7, Section 686a subsection 4(b) BW).

2.2 Possible applications by the employee after the employment contract has been set aside

2.2.1 Reinstatement of the employment contract

After the sub-district court has set aside the employment contract, the employee can apply for **reinstatement of his/her employment contract** due to breach of the condition for recommencement of employment (Book 7, Section 682 subsection 4 and subsection 5 BW). Note that the condition for recommencement of employment only applies if the employment contract was set aside pursuant to Book 7, Section 669 subsection 3(a) BW (discontinuation of the operations or business economic reasons). This application must be submitted to the court within two months after the date on which the employment contract was set aside (Book 7, Section 686a subsection 4(c) BW). The employee can also apply for fair compensation instead of reinstatement (Book 7, Section 682 subsections

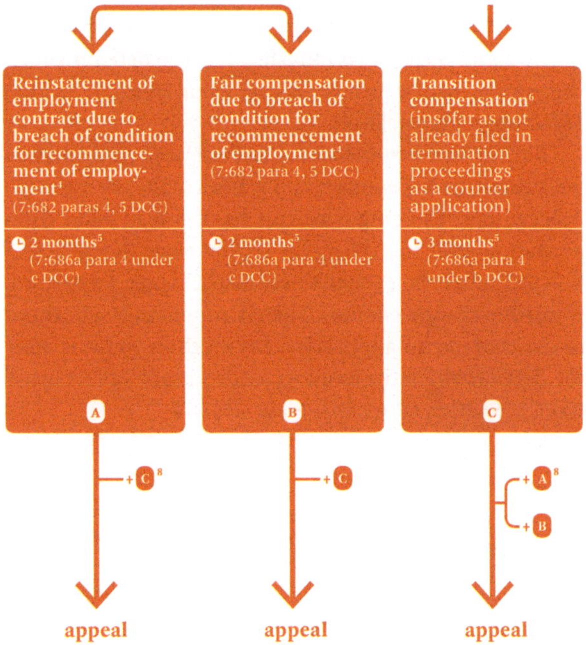
Reinstatement of employment contract due to breach of condition for recommencement of employment[4]
(7:682 paras 4, 5 DCC)
2 months[5]
(7:686a para 4 under c DCC)
A
Fair compensation due to breach of condition for recommencement of employment[4]
(7:682 para 4, 5 DCC)
2 months[5]
(7:686a para 4 under c DCC)
B
Transition compensation[6] (insofar as not already filed in termination proceedings as a counter application)
3 months[5]
(7:686a para 4 under b DCC)
C
+C[8]
+C
+A[8]
+B
appeal
appeal
appeal

4 and 5 BW). The employee must submit this application to the court within two months after the date on which the employment contract was set aside (Book 7, Section 686a subsection 4(c) BW).

If transition compensation has not been paid and was not submitted as a counter-application in the setting aside proceedings, the employee can request transition compensation after the ruling on setting aside (Book 7, Section 673 subsection 1(a) BW) (see also Chapter 3 regarding transition compensation). The claim must be submitted to the court in an application within three months after the date on which the employment contract was set aside (Book 7, Section 686a subsection 4(b) BW).

Chapter 3
Employee compensation

3.1 Transition compensation

If the employment contract is terminated, set aside or not extended on the employer's initiative, from 1 July 2015, the employee is entitled to transition compensation (Book 7, Section 673 BW). The employee is also entitled to transition compensation if the employment contract is terminated, set aside or not extended by the employee as a result of serious imputable acts or omissions on the part of the employer. No transition compensation will be due if the employment contract was terminated by mutual consent. In practice, however, it will not happen often that an employee agrees to termination of his/her employment contract by mutual consent if transition compensation is not offered at the very least. Transition compensation is only payable if the employment contract lasts at least 24 months. Transition compensation is intended as compensation for dismissal and is intended to facilitate the employee's transition to another job.

Transition compensation is calculated as follows:

a. for the first 120 months of the employment contract: 1/6 monthly salary for each period of 6 months that the employment contract has lasted;
b. after the first 120 months: 1/4 monthly salary for each subsequent period of 6 months.

Since 1 July 2015 the amount of transition compensation has been capped at EUR 75,000 gross or – if the employee is entitled to a higher annual salary – at one gross annual salary. As of 1 January 2016, the EUR 75,000 gross cap will be raised to a maximum of EUR 76,000 gross.[78] Calculation of the gross monthly salary is based on the agreed gross hourly salary multiplied by the agreed number of working hours per month. This is done as much as possible in line with the previously applicable 'B factor' in the 'sub-district court formula'. Until 1 July 2015, this formula was used to calculate dismissal compensation when employment contracts were set aside. The 'B factor' comprised the gross monthly salary plus agreed fixed salary components, such as holiday allowance, a fixed thirteenth month, a structural overtime allowance and a fixed shift allowance. These salary components also count in the transition compensation, on the understanding that an overtime allowance does not need to be structural.

Example
A 45-year-old employee with 15 years and 7 months of service and a gross salary of EUR 3,000 including holiday allowance receives the following transition compensation as a result of reorganisation. The first 10 years of service result in an amount of 1/6 monthly salary per half year, thus 20 x 3,000 x 1/6 = EUR 10,000. For the subsequent years of service, the employee receives 1/4 monthly salary per half year of service, thus 11 x 3,000 x 1/4 = EUR

78 See the Regulations of the Minister of Social Affairs and Employment of 21 September 2015, Government Gazette 31852.

8,250. The total transition compensation then amounts to 10,000 + 8,250 = EUR 18,250 gross.

The employer may deduct the following costs from the transition compensation:

a. Any transition compensation paid earlier on termination of a prior employment contract.
b. Costs of measures in connection with ending or not continuing the employment contract aimed at preventing unemployment or shortening the period of joblessness. Under the 'Transitional Compensation (Conditions for Deduction of Costs) Decree' ('*Besluit voorwaarden in mindering brengen kosten op transitievergoeding*'),[79] these are called **transition costs.** In order to deduct these costs from the transition compensation, these costs must (i) be incurred after these costs were specified and communicated to the employee in writing; (ii) be incurred after the employee consented in writing to deduction of the specified costs; (iii) be incurred by the employer who owes transition compensation for the benefit of the employee to whom transition compensation is owed; (iv) not relate to the employee's salary; (v) be in reasonable proportion to the purpose for which these costs were incurred; (vi) have been or will be incurred during or after the period on which the transaction compensation is calculated; (vii) not be recoverable from a third party; and (viii) not be recoverable from the

79 See the Transitional Compensation (Conditions for Deduction of Costs) Decree (*Besluit voorwaarden in mindering brengen kosten op transitievergoeding*) of 23 April 2015, Bulletin of Acts and Decrees 2015, 171.

employee. Transaction costs would include the costs of training or retraining, an outplacement procedure on dismissal or the costs of observing a longer notice period than the statutory notional notice period (provided the employee has been exempted from work).

c. Costs in relation to facilitating the broader employability of the employee that were incurred during or on termination or not continuing the employment contract. These are the so-called **employability costs.** These costs must also meet the abovementioned conditions (i to viii) in order to qualify for deduction from the transition compensation. These costs must also be incurred to facilitate the employability of the employee outside the employer's organisation. In addition, these costs must be incurred in the period of five years prior to the date on which the transition compensation is due, unless the employer and employee have agreed otherwise in writing. Employability costs can also be the costs of dual training courses.

No transitional compensation is due if the employment contract ends or a decision not to continue it is taken:

a. before the date on which the employee has reached the age of 18 and the average number of hours worked was 12 hours a week at most;
b. after employee has reached retirement age;
c. due to serious imputable acts or omissions on the part of the employee. Here we have in mind theft, embezzlement, fraud or other serious offences through which the employee loses the employer's trust, the employee frequently and without a well-founded reason arriving late for work, the business

operations are hindered by this and the employer has already called the employee to account for this in vain.

The basic assumption is that transition compensation always has to be paid, even if the employer is in very bad business economic circumstances.

Transitional compensation is not due if the employer (i) has been declared insolvent; or (ii) has been granted suspension of payment; or (iii) the debt management scheme for natural persons has been declared applicable to it.

3.1.1 Transition compensation under transitional law

The legislature has provided for transitional law under the 'Transition Compensation (Transitional Law) Decree' ('*Besluit overgangsrecht transitievergoeding*').[80] In brief, this decree lays down how employers must deal with agreements on 'compensation and provisions' on dismissal that were entered into before 1 July 2015. These are dealt with in a social plan, collective labour agreement or directly with the individual employee him/herself. The starting point is that the employer is not obliged to make double payments.

This transitional law applies to compensation and provisions that were entered into before 1 July 2015 and from which rights can be derived on 1 July 2015.

80 See the Transition Compensation (Transitional Law) Decree (*Besluit voorwaarden in mindering brengen kosten op transitievergoeding*) of 23 April 2015, Bulletin of Acts and Decrees 2015, 172.

'Compensation' means, for example, dismissal compensation. The term 'provisions' includes all agreements not relating to compensation, such as agreements on an outplacement procedure, retraining or additional training or a redundancy pay scheme.

The general rule is that agreements made with an employees' association (for example in a collective labour agreement or social plan), in which no account is taken of the statutory transition compensation, take precedence over the transition compensation. This transitional arrangement continues to apply until the agreements made with an employees' association have been extended or amended, and until 1 July 2016 at the latest. The transitional law will also continue to apply if the employment contract ends on or after 1 July 2016, but the procedure at UWV or the sub-district court started before 1 May 2016. The transitional arrangement also applies if the collective labour agreement remains in effect or is tacitly extended.

For other agreements (for example in the individual employment contract or with the works council), the employee has to choose between the statutory transition compensation and his/her right to compensation or provisions under previous agreements. The end date of 1 July 2016 is not relevant here. This transitional rule applies as long as the employee can derive rights from the agreements.

3.1.2 Transition compensation and older employees

There is also a transitional arrangement for older employees. The underlying idea of this arrangement is that older employees are always in a worse position on the labour market. An employee who is 50 years of age or older and has been in the employer's service for at least 10 years is therefore entitled to transition compensation of half a monthly salary per year of service counting from his/her 50th birthday. With that, an attempt is made to compensate older employees and to prevent employers from dismissing older employees too readily, as it has become much cheaper under the new dismissal compensation law. This arrangement does not apply to small companies (fewer than 25 employees) and to employers to be designated by the minister. This arrangement will cease to apply as of 1 January 2020.

With the entry into effect of transition compensation and disappearance of the sub-district court formula, the amount of the transition compensation seems to be normative for determining the amount of compensation if the parties wish to take leave of each other by mutual consent. It is self-evident that a higher offer will have to be made to get an employee to agree to termination by mutual consent. He/she will want to be compensated for the lack of a possibility of appeal or appeal in cassation, and the employer will want to encourage the employee to disregard the 14-day reflection period within which the employee can cancel the termination agreement (out of court). Please note that the reflection period cannot be done away with by contract.

If the employer has not paid transition compensation, the employee can request transition compensation pursuant to Book 7, Section 673 subsection 1(a)(1) BW. That claim must be submitted to the sub-district court in an application within two months after the date on which the employment contract was set aside (Book 7, Section 686a subsection 4(a)(1) BW). Please note that the aforementioned period will be three months if the employment contract was terminated after consent by the employee and in the case of a director or officer of a legal entity not being a foundation (Book 7, Section 686a subsection 4(b) BW). An employee whose contract is terminated owing to the state pension or different retirement age being reached is not entitled to transition compensation.[81]

3.2 Fair compensation (Book 7, Section 681 subsection 1(a-e) BW, Book 7, Section 682 subsection 4 and subsection 5)

In exceptional cases the employee will also have a right (as well) to fair compensation in addition to transition compensation. The possibility of this additional fair compensation is laid down in several provisions of the Dutch Civil Code and can be awarded in most cases only in the event of 'serious imputable acts or omissions' of the employer. Practice will have to show exactly what comes under this.[82]

It concerns the following situations:

a. Termination of the employment contract at the request of the employer (pursuant to Book 7, Section 671b subsection 8(c) and subsection 9(b) BW).

81 See also: *Parliamentary Papers II* 2013/14, 33818, no. 3, p. 39.

82 See also: P. Kruit, 'De ontslagvergoeding: transitie van billijkheid naar forfaitair, of toch weer billijkheid?', *Tijdschrift voor Arbeidsrechtpraktijk* 2014; K. Hakvoort and P. Kruit, '(Ontslag)vergoedingen onder de WWZ: hoe goedkoop is de WWZ voor de verwijtbare werkgever?', *Tijdschrift voor Arbeidsrechtpraktijk* 2015/226; S.F. Sagel, 'Werk en zekerheid: ontslagrecht doen in tijden van hard en fast rules', (Oration 5 September 2014, Leiden University).

b. Termination at the request of the employee (pursuant to Book 7, Section 671c subsection 2(b) and subsection 3(b) BW).
c. Termination in conflict with the a or b ground after permission has been given by the UWV and the employee does not want reinstatement of the employment (pursuant to Book 7, Section 682 subsection 1 (b and c) BW).
d. Not extending a fixed-term employment contract (pursuant to Book 7, Section 673 subsection 9 BW).

The fair compensation to be awarded is related to the serious imputable acts or omissions committed by the employer. Consequently there is no room in the fair compensation to take into account any adverse (financial) consequences of a dismissal for the employee, as was indeed possible in the sub-district court formula.

Besides the fair compensation due to 'serious imputable acts or omissions by the employer', Book 7, Sections 681 and 682 subsection 3(a), subsection 4(b) and subsection 5(b) also contain fair compensation. No serious imputable acts or omissions on the part of the employer are required for this fair compensation, so it is possible to claim this fair compensation in addition to the abovementioned fair compensation. The latter fair compensation can be awarded by the court in case of (i) voidable termination; (ii) termination of a director or officer under the articles of association without a reasonable ground; and (iii) breach of the abovementioned condition for recommencement of employment.

3.3 Compensation for defective termination (Book 7, Section 672 subsection 9 and subsection 10 BW)

If the employer terminates the employment contract without observing the applicable notice period, if a notice period must be observed, the employee can submit an application for compensation due to defective termination. The compensation amounts to the sum of the wages for the period that the employment contract should have continued in case of regular termination. The sub-district court judge can mitigate the compensation.

Chapter 4
Appeal and appeal in cassation (Book 7, Section 683 BW)

With the new legislation, a system has been chosen in which all court proceedings (in the first instance) start by submitting an application to the sub-district court. What is new is the possibility to bring an appeal and an appeal in cassation against sub-district court decisions. Bringing an appeal does not suspend enforcement of the decision in the first instance. If the court allows the appeal against the sub-district court decision, which may result in the employment contract still existing or having to be reinstated, the court can always award the employee fair compensation instead of doing so ex officio. If the case concerns a setting aside at the request of the employee that has been allowed, the employer can only appeal against the compensation awarded in this, if applicable. After all, this would otherwise result in forced labour.

Appeals are lodged by filing a notice of appeal. The expiry period for filing the notice of appeal is two months from the end of the employment contract, except for proceedings in connection with transition compensation to which an expiry period of three months from the end of the employment contract applies. Any interested party can file a statement of defence under the applicable law of civil procedure. The interested party or parties called up on appeal must file the statement of defence within four weeks of a copy of the notice of appeal being sent to them, unless the court will rule against it.[83]

83 See also: P.G. Vestering en W.J.J. Wetzels, *Praktisch arbeidsprocesrecht onder de WWZ*, The Hague: Sdu Uitgevers 2015.

Scenarios

Routes

Under the Dutch Work and Security Act (WWZ) the reason for dismissal is decisive for the dismissal route that can or must be followed. The following scenarios, among others, may be reasons for an employer's intention to dismiss.

- **Business closure**
Example: end of all activities of the undertaking

- **Economic circumstances**
Example: axing of one or more jobs due to poor financial results or a reorganisation aimed at achieving efficiency.

- **Long-term illness**
Example: employee is sick for longer than 104 weeks and it is unlikely that there will be any recovery within 26 weeks or that the employee can be reassigned to a suitable alternative position within 26 weeks.

- **Frequent sickness absence**
Example: frequent sickness absence that leads to unacceptable consequences for the undertakings' business operations.

- **Inadequate performance**
Example: employee is unsuitable for the performance of the work. The employer has given the employee due notice of his/her inadequate performance and the opportunity to improve it, but this has failed to produce any results.

- **Culpable acts or omissions of the employee**
Example: a sick employee does not comply with statutory reintegration obligations. The employer has given the employee a written demand to comply and/or stopped payment of wages.

N.B. This ground is broader than the urgent cause for instant dismissal but under certain circumstances, the culpable acts or omissions of the employee can also constitute urgent cause. On the other hand, culpability is not always needed for urgent cause.

- **Refusal to perform the stipulated work due to a serious conscientious objection**
Examples: not wishing to cooperate in the construction of roads through nature conservation areas or the construction of a nuclear power station.

- **Damaged working relationship**
Example: incompatibility of temperament, the employer and employee can no longer work under one roof with each other even though there is no question of inadequate performance and the damaged working relationship is not wholly due to the employer's actions.

- **Termination during probationary period**
Examples: the employee does not fit within the team or the employee's performance does not meet the job requirements and the employer terminates the employment contract within the valid probationary period that has been agreed in writing.

- **Termination of relationship under employment and corporate law with the director of a legal entity, other than a foundation**
Examples: difference of opinion on the strategy to be adopted, organisational or economic reasons.

- **Termination for urgent cause (instant dismissal)**
Examples: fraud, forgery, drunkenness, theft, embezzlement, gross neglect of the obligations under the employment contract.

N.B. As culpability of the employee is not always required for urgent cause, termination cannot always also be on ground e.

- **Refusal of permission from the Employee Insurance Agency (UWV) or collective labour agreement (CLA) committee to terminate the employment contract**
Example: a request for permission to terminate the employment contract for organisational reasons is refused by the UWV or CLA committee.

- **Dismissal of the employee due to insolvency**
Example: the employment contract with the employee must be terminated by the liquidator because the employer is insolvent.

- **Termination due to other circumstances**
Examples: illegality, detention, not being in possession of a work permit, or a difference of opinion on the policy to be adopted.

Notes accompanying flowcharts

1. The employee does not have this right if he/she consents in writing to termination or enters into a written termination agreement within six months of an earlier revocation or termination (7:671 para 5 and 7:670b para 4 DCC (DCC = Dutch Civil Code)). A director of a legal entity, other than a foundation, has no right of termination (7:670b para 5 DCC).
2. After the date of the written consent or written termination agreement. The period is three weeks if the employer does not refer the employee, within two working days of the consent or the termination agreement, to the right of revocation or the right of termination.
3. If the employee files an application for the notice of termination to be nullied, the employer may file a counter application under certain circumstances for conditional termination on the basis of grounds c-h of 7:669 para 3 DCC or make a request to the UWV for conditional consent on grounds a-b of 7:669 para 3 DCC.
4. The condition for recommencement of employment applies only if there has been termination or setting aside on the basis of 7:669 para 3 under a DCC.
5. After the day on which the employment contract ends.
6. The employer owes compensation for defective termination and/or transition compensation by operation of law. If the employer does not pay, the employee will have to file an application with the subdistrict court.
7. After the date of the permission.
8. The explanatory memorandum (p. 39) assumes that transition compensation is not due in case of reinstatement with retroactive effect. However, this is inconsistent with the law.

After all, the employment contract has been legally terminated at the employer's initiative.

9. After the day on which the UWV or CLA committee has refused permission.
10. With whom the employment contract is entered into before reaching that age.

Book 7 of the Dutch Civil Code (DCC)

Book 7, Section 652

1. If the parties have agreed a probationary period, it is equal for both parties.
2. The probationary period is agreed in writing.
3. When entering into an indefinite employment contract, the agreed probationary period may not exceed two months.
4. A probationary period may not be agreed if the term of the employment contract does not exceed six months.
5. When entering into a fixed-term employment contract for longer than six months, the agreed probationary period may not exceed:
a. one month if the term of the contract is less than two years;
b. two months if the term of the contract is two years or longer.
6. If a calendar date has not been set for the end of a fixed-term employment contract, the agreed probationary period may not exceed one month.
7. Derogation from paragraphs 5, sub-paragraph a, and 6 to the employee's detriment is possible only based on a collective labour agreement or a regulation made by or on behalf of a competent management body.
8. Any stipulation by which a probationary period is agreed is invalid if:
a. the probationary period is not equal for both parties;

b. the probationary period, other than by means of a collective labour agreement or a regulation made by or on behalf of a competent management body, is longer than one month in the case referred to in paragraph 5, sub-paragraph a;
c. the probationary period is longer than two months;
d. the stipulation is included in a subsequent employment contract between an employee and the same employer, unless the contract clearly requires different skills or responsibilities of the employee than the earlier employment contract does;
e. the stipulation is included in a subsequent employment contract between an employee and a different employer, which, with regard to the work performed, can reasonably be deemed to be the successor of the former employer; or
f. the stipulation is included in an employment contract with a maximum term of six months.

Section 9. End of the employment contract

Book 7, Section 667

1. An employment contract ends by operation of law when the period stipulated in the contract or by law has expired.
2. Prior notice of termination is required:
a. if it has been stipulated in a written contract;
b. if notice is required by law or common practice and there is no written agreement permitting this that stipulates otherwise.
3. An employment contract as referred to in paragraph 1 may be terminated early only if it has been agreed in writing by each of the parties.
4. If an indefinite employment contract that has been terminated other than through notice of termination as referred to in Section 671, paragraph 1, sub-paragraphs a - h, Section 40 of the Dutch Bankruptcy Act (*Faillissementswet*), or set aside by the court, or is followed immediately or after an interval of no

more than six months by a fixed-term employment contract, notice of termination is needed, notwithstanding paragraph 1, for the termination of that successive employment contract. The notice period is calculated from the date on which the indefinite employment contract is concluded. This paragraph does not apply if the indefinite employment contract is terminated because the employee has reached retirement age under a stipulation to that effect.

5. Successive employment contracts as referred to in paragraph 4 also exist if the same employee is successively employed at different employers that, regardless of whether there is insight into the capacity and suitability of the employee, must reasonably be deemed to be each other's successor with regard to the work performed.

6. Prior notice of termination is required for the termination of an indefinite employment contract.

7. A stipulation by which the employment contract ends by operation of law if the employee marries or enters into a registered partnership is invalid.

8. A stipulation by which the employment contract ends by operation of law if the employee falls pregnant or gives birth is invalid.

Book 7, Section 668

1. The employer must inform the employee in writing, no later than one month before a fixed-term employment contract ends:

a. whether or not the employment contract will be renewed; and

b. in the event of renewal, the conditions under which it wishes to continue the employment contract.

2. Paragraph 1 does not apply if:

a. it was agreed in writing when the employment contract was concluded that it would end at a time that has not been set to a calendar date; or

b. the employment contract was entered into for a period of less than six months.

3. If the employer has not complied fully with the obligation referred to in paragraph 1, preamble and sub-paragraph a, it must pay the employee compensation equal to one month's wages. If the employer does not comply with that obligation on time, it must pay the employee pro-rata compensation. The compensation is no longer due if the employer is declared insolvent, is granted a moratorium on the payment of debts, or if the statutory debt management scheme for natural persons is declared applicable to him/her.

4. The employment contract will be deemed to be renewed for the same period, but for no more than one year, on the basis of its earlier conditions if:

a. the employment contract referred to in paragraph 1 is renewed after the expiry of the period referred to in Section 667, paragraph 1 and the employer has not complied with the obligation referred to in paragraph 1, sub-paragraph a or b; or

b. the employment contract referred to in paragraph 2 is renewed by the parties without any objections, after the expiry of the period referred to in Section 667, paragraph 1.

5. Paragraph 4, sub-paragraph b also applies in cases in which notice of termination is required, punctual notice of termination is not forthcoming, and the consequences of renewing the employment contract have not been expressly catered for.

6. The meaning of wage for the purpose of paragraph 3 will be determined by means of or pursuant to an order in council.

Book 7, Section 668a

1. From the date on which the same parties:

a. have had successive fixed-term employment contracts with each other with intervals not exceeding six months, and that have exceeded a period of 24 months, including these intervals, the last employment contract will be regarded as an indefinite employment contract from that date;

b. have had more than three successive fixed-term employment contracts with each other with intervals not exceeding six months, the last employment contract will be regarded as an indefinite employment contract.

2. Paragraph 1 applies mutatis mutandis to successive employment contracts between an employee and different employers, which, regardless of whether there is insight into the capacity and suitability of the employee, must reasonably be deemed to be each other's successor with regard to the work performed.

3. Paragraph 1, sub-paragraph a does not apply to an employment contract entered into for no more than three months that immediately succeeds an employment contract entered into between the same parties for 24 months or longer.

4. The notice period is calculated from the time of entering into the first employment contract as referred to under a or b of paragraph 1.

5. The period of 24 months referred to in paragraph 1 sub-paragraph a may be extended, based on a collective labour agreement or a regulation made by or on behalf of a competent management body, to a maximum of 48 months and the three months referred to in paragraph 1, sub-paragraph b may be increased to a maximum of six, if:

a. the contract is a temporary employment contract as referred to in Section 690; or

b. it is clear from that contract or regulation that this extension or increase is required for the jobs or job categories determined in that contract or regulation and for the intrinsic nature of the business operations.

6. Derogation from paragraph 2 to the employee's detriment is possible based on a collective labour agreement or a regulation made by or on behalf of a competent management body.

7. Derogation from the period referred to in paragraph 1, subparagraph a to the detriment of a director of a legal entity is possible based on a written agreement or a regulation made by or on behalf of a competent management body.
8. This article may be declared inapplicable, based on a collective labour agreement or a regulation made by or on behalf of a competent management body, for certain jobs in a business sector if the Dutch Minister of Social Affairs and Employment has designated these jobs under a ministerial regulation because it is established practice for those jobs in that business sector and essential because of the intrinsic nature of the business operations, and those jobs for work to be performed exclusively on the basis of fixed-term employment contracts that are not temporary employment contracts as referred to in Section 690. Under this regulation, further conditions can be set for the declaration of inapplicability as referred to in the first sentence.
9. This section may be declared fully or partially inapplicable, based on a collective labour agreement or regulation made by or on behalf of a competent management body, to the employment contracts designated therein that are exclusively or mainly entered into for the benefit of the employee's education.
10. This section does not apply to employment contracts that are entered into with regard to vocational training as referred to in Section 7.2.2. of the Dutch Adult and Vocational Education Act (*Wet educatie en beroepsonderwijs*).
11. This section does not apply to an employment contract with an employee who has not yet reached the age of eighteen, if the average extent of the work performed by him/her has not exceeded twelve hours a week.

Book 7, Section 669

1. The employer may give notice of termination of the employment contract if a reasonable ground for this exists and if

reassignment of the employee within a reasonable period to a suitable alternative position, with the help of training or otherwise, is not possible or is not logical. Reassignment is not logical in any case if the employee has acted or failed to act in an imputable manner as referred to in paragraph 3, sub-paragraph e.

2. Reassignment as referred to in paragraph 1 is not required if the employee holds a ministry.

3. A reasonable ground as referred to in paragraph 1 includes:

a. redundancies due to termination of the company's operations or, viewed over a future period of at least 26 weeks, necessary job cuts due to the adoption of measures for effective business operations due to economic circumstances;

b. the illness or disability of the employee as a result of which he/she is no longer able to perform the stipulated work, provided that the period referred to in Section 670, paragraphs 1 and 11 has expired, and it is unlikely that there will be any recovery within 26 weeks or that the work can be performed in an adapted form;

c. the regular inability to perform the stipulated work as a result of illness or disability of the employee with unacceptable consequences for business operations, provided that such regular inability to perform the stipulated work is not the result of the employer not taking sufficient care to ensure that the employee's working conditions are adequate; it is unlikely that there will be any recovery within 26 weeks or that the work can be performed in an adapted form within that period;

d. the unsuitability of the employee to perform the stipulated work, other than as a result of his/her illness or disability, provided that the employer has given the employee due notice thereof and adequate opportunity to improve his/her performance, and the unsuitability is not the result of the employer not taking sufficient care to ensure that the employee's training or working conditions are adequate;

e. imputable acts or omissions on the part of the employee, such that the employer cannot reasonably be required to allow the employment contract to continue;
f. the refusal of the employee to perform the stipulated work due to a serious conscientious objection, provided that it is unlikely that the work can be performed in an adapted form;
g. a disrupted working relationship, such that the employer cannot reasonably be required to allow the employment contract to continue;
h. circumstances other than the above, such that the employer cannot reasonably be required to allow the employment contract to continue.
4. Unless otherwise agreed in writing, the employer may also give notice of termination of the employment contract with effect from or after the date on which the employee reaches the age referred to in Section 7a, paragraph 1 of the General Old Age Pensions Act (*Algemene Ouderdomswet*) or, if a different retirement age applies to the employee, the age at which his/her entitlement to pension is reached, if the employment contract is entered into prior to reaching that age.
5. Based on a regulation of the Minister of Social Affairs and Employment:
a. further rules are set with regard to a reasonable ground for termination, the reassignment of an employee, and the reasonable period as referred to in paragraph 1, by which a distinction may be made according to categories of employees;
b. rules are set to determine the order in which notices of termination are to be given for redundancies as referred to in paragraph 3, sub-paragraph a.
6. The rules referred to in paragraph 5, sub-paragraph b do not apply if other rules are set, based on a collective labour agreement or a regulation made by or on behalf of a competent management body, for determining the order in which notices of

termination are to be given in case of redundancies as referred to in paragraph 3, sub-paragraph a, and an independent committee as referred to in Section 671a, paragraph 2 is appointed.
7. This section does not apply to a notice of termination during the probationary period.

Book 7, Section 670

1. The employer may not give a notice of termination during the period that the employee is incapacitated for work due to illness, unless the incapacity for work:
a. has lasted at least two years; or
b. commenced after a request for approval as referred to in Section 671a has been received by the Employee Insurance Agency (*Uitvoeringsinstituut werknemersverzekeringen*) or the committee as referred to in Section 671a, paragraph 2.
In order to calculate the period as referred to in sub-paragraph a, periods of incapacity for work as a result of pregnancy prior to maternity leave and periods of incapacity for work during maternity leave as referred to in Section 3:1, paragraphs 2 and 3 of the Dutch Work and Care Act (*Wet arbeid en zorg*) are not taken into account. Periods of incapacity for work, other than those referred to in the previous sentence, are furthermore added together if they succeed each other with an interruption of less than four weeks, or if they are immediately prior to and following a period in which maternity leave is taken in accordance with Section 3:1, paragraphs 2 and 3 of the Dutch Work and Care Act, unless the incapacity for work cannot be deemed to arise from the same cause.
2. The employer may not give the employee notice of termination of the employment during pregnancy. The employer may require proof of the pregnancy based on a certificate from a physician or obstetrician. The employer may not give notice of termination of the employee's employment contract during the period in

which she is on maternity leave as referred to in Section 3:1, paragraph 3 of the Dutch Work and Care Act and after she resumes work for a period of six weeks following that maternity leave, or following a period of incapacity for work due to the childbirth or the preceding pregnancy and which follows that maternity leave. The employer may not give notice of termination of the employee's employment contract during the period that he/she is on leave as referred to in Section 3:1a, paragraphs 1 or 4 of the Dutch Work and Care Act.

3. The employer may not give notice of termination when the employee is prevented from performing the stipulated work because he/she has been called up as a conscript for military or alternative service.

4. The employer may not give notice of termination of the employment contract with an employee who is a member of:

1. a works council, central works council, group works council, a permanent committee of those councils, a subcommittee of the works council, or an employee representative body;

2. a special negotiation body or a European works council as referred to in the European Works Councils Act, or who acts legally as some other kind of representative for providing information to and consulting employees;

3. a special negotiation body, an SE (*Societas Europeae* or European company) works council or if the employee representative is a member of the supervisory or executive body of the European company as referred to in Chapter 1 of the Employee Involvement (European Companies) Act, or acts legally as a representative in some other form of providing information to and consultation of employees;

4. a special negotiation body, an SCE (*Societas Cooperativa Europaea*) works council or if the employee representative is a member of the supervisory or executive body of the European Cooperative Society (SE) as referred to in Chapter 2 of the

Employee Involvement (European Companies) Act, or acts pursuant to Chapter 2 of that Act as some other kind of representative for providing information to and consulting employees.
If the employer includes a secretary in the works council or employee representation, the first sentence applies mutatis mutandis to that secretary. If the employer includes a secretary to the works council, the first sentence of this paragraph applies mutatis mutandis to that secretary.
5. The employer may not give notice of termination of the employment contract because the employee is a member of an association of employees whose purpose, in accordance with its articles of association, is to represent the interests of the members as employees, or due to performing or participating in activities for that association, unless the activities are performed during working hours without the employer's permission.
6. The employer may not give an employee notice of termination of the employment contract because he/she attends meetings as referred to in Section 643 if the employee has been given leave to do so. The same applies if the parties have not agreed on the leave as long as the court has not ruled thereon.
7. The employer may not give notice of termination of the employment contract because the employee enforces his/her right to leave as referred to in Section 3:1a, paragraph 1 or 4 of the Dutch Work and Care Act, his/her right to adoption leave or leave for fostering a child as referred to in Section 3:2 of the Dutch Work and Care Act, to short- or long-term carer's leave as referred to in Section 5 of the Dutch Work and Care Act, or his/her right to parental leave as referred to in Section 6 of the Dutch Work and Care Act.
8. The employer may not give notice of termination of the employment contract to an employee working in its company due to the transfer of that company as referred to in Section 662, paragraph 2, sub-paragraph a.

9. The employer may not give notice of termination of the employment contract because the employee does not agree to work on Sundays as referred to in Section 5:6, paragraph 2, second sentence or paragraph 4, second sentence of the Dutch Working Hours Act (*Arbeidstijdenwet*).
10. The employer may not give notice of termination of the employment contract to an employee who:
a. is placed on a list of candidates for a works council or employee representation body, or was a member less than two years previously of a works council, central works council, group works council or committee of those councils, an employee representative body, special negotiation body, a European works council, SE works council or SCE works council as referred to in the European Works Councils Act or Chapter 1 or 2 of the Employee Involvement (European Companies) Act, or who acted as some other kind of representative less than two years previously under one of those Acts for providing information to and consulting employees;
b. is a member of a preparatory committee of a works council, central works council or group works council;
c. works as an expert employee as referred to in Section 13, paragraphs 1 and 2 of the Dutch Working Conditions Act (*Arbeidsomstandighedenwet*) or as an expert person as referred to in Section 14, paragraph 1, of that Act; or
d. works as a data protection officer as referred to in Section 62 of the Dutch Personal Data Protection Act (*Wet bescherming persoonsgegevens*).
11. The two-year period referred to in paragraph 1, sub-paragraph a will be extended:
a. by the length of the delay if the application as referred to in Section 64, paragraph 1, of the Dutch Work and Income (Capacity for Work) Act (*Wet werk en inkomen naar arbeidsvermogen*) is made later than is prescribed in or on the basis of that section;

b. by the length of the extension of the waiting period as referred to in Section 19, paragraph 1 of the Dutch Invalidity Insurance Act (*Wet op de arbeidsongeschiktheidsverzekering*) if that waiting period is extended on the basis of paragraph 7 of that section; and

c. by the length of the period that the Employee Insurance Agency has determined on the basis of Section 24, paragraph 1, or Section 25, paragraph 9 of the Dutch Work and Income (Capacity for Work) Act or on the basis of Section 71a, paragraph 9 of the Dutch Invalidity Insurance Act.

12. For the purpose of paragraph 4 and paragraph 10, the term 'SE works council' means the body that represents employees in a European company (SE) that has its registered office in another Member State, and that is established pursuant to the provisions of the national law of that Member State for the transposition of Council Directive 2001/86/EC of 8 October 2001 supplementing the Statute for a European company with regard to the involvement of employees (OJEC L 294).

13. For the purpose of paragraph 4 and paragraph 10, the term 'SCE works council' means the body that represents employees in a European cooperative society (SE) that has its registered office in another Member State, and that is established pursuant to the provisions of the national law of that Member State for the transposition of Council Directive 2003/72/EC of 22 July 2003 supplementing the Statute for a European Cooperative Society with regard to the involvement of employees (OJEC L 207).

14. Derogation from paragraph 3 is possible only based on a collective labour agreement or a regulation made by or on behalf of a competent management body.

Book 7, Section 670a

1. Section 670, paragraph 1, sub-paragraph a does not apply if the employee refuses without proper cause to comply with the

obligations as referred to in Section 660a, and the employer has demanded compliance of those obligations in writing from the employee or for that reason, and with due observance of the provisions of Section 629, paragraph 7, has suspended the payment of wages.

2. Section 670, paragraphs 1 to 4 and paragraph 10, and prohibitions on termination in another legal provision that are comparable by nature and purport do not apply if:

a. the employee has agreed in writing to the notice of termination;

b. the notice of termination is given during the probationary period;

c. the notice of termination is given on the basis of Section 677, paragraph 1;

d. the notice of termination is given due to the ending of the company's activities, on the understanding that the notice of termination cannot affect an employee who is on maternity leave as referred to in Section 3:1 of the Dutch Work and Care Act; or

e. the notice of termination is given on the basis of Section 669, paragraph 4, insofar as the notice of termination does not relate to circumstances to which the prohibitions on termination apply.

3. If the notice of termination is given on the basis of Section 669, paragraph 3, sub-paragraph a, other than because of the end of the company's activities, and the employee has been working at least 26 weeks in the job that is being made redundant:

a. Section 670, paragraph 2 does not apply if the activities of the company in which the employee exclusively or mainly works end, on the understanding that the notice of termination cannot affect an employee who is on maternity leave as referred to in Section 3:1 of the Dutch Work and Care Act;

b. Section 670, paragraph 3 does not apply if the activities of the company in which the employee exclusively or mainly works end;

c. Section 670, paragraphs 4 and 10 do not apply.
4. Paragraph 3 applies mutatis mutandis to prohibitions on termination that are comparable by nature and purport with those referred to in paragraph 3.
5. The employee is entitled to revoke his/her agreement, as referred to in paragraph 2, sub-paragraph a, within 14 days of the date thereof and without giving reasons based on a written declaration addressed to the employer.
6. Section 671, paragraphs 3 - 6 apply mutatis mutandis to the written consent as referred to in paragraph 2, sub-paragraph a.
7. Paragraphs 5 and 6 do not apply to the director of a legal entity if it is not possible to reinstate the employment contract on the basis of Book 2 of the Dutch Civil Code, or to the director of a comparable foreign legal entity.
8. Any stipulation by which the right as referred to in paragraph 5 is excluded or limited is invalid.

Book 7, Section 670b

1. An agreement by which an employment contract is terminated is only valid if it is entered into in writing.
2. If the employment contract is terminated based on a written agreement, the employee is entitled to terminate this agreement, without giving reasons, within 14 days of the date on which it was concluded based on a written declaration addressed to the employer.
3. The employer must mention the right referred to in paragraph 2 in the contract referred to in paragraph 1, failing which the period referred to in paragraph 2 will be three weeks.
4. Paragraphs 2 and 3 do not apply if the parties enter into a new agreement as referred to in paragraph 1 within six months of a termination as referred to in paragraph 2 or a revocation as referred to in Section 671, paragraph 2.

5. Paragraphs 2 to 4 do not apply to the director of a legal entity if it is not possible to reinstate the employment contract on the basis of Book 2 of the Dutch Civil Code, or to the director of a comparable foreign legal entity.
6. Any stipulation by which the right as referred to in paragraph 2 is excluded or limited is invalid.

Book 7, Section 671

1. The employer may not validly give notice of termination of the employment contract without the employee's written agreement, unless:
a. agreement as referred to in Section 671a has been given for the termination;
b. the notice of termination is given during the probationary period;
c. the notice of termination is given on the basis of Section 677, paragraph 1;
d. the notice of termination relates to an employee who usually works for less than four days a week exclusively or practically exclusively for the household of the natural persons by whom he/she is employed, which work also includes providing care to the members of that household;
e. the notice of termination relates to the director of a legal entity whose employment contract cannot be reinstated on the basis of Book 2 of the Dutch Civil Code, or to the director of a comparable foreign legal entity;
f. the notice of termination relates to an employee who holds a ministry;
g. the notice of termination is given on the basis of Section 669, paragraph 4; or
h. the notice of termination relates to an employee who works at a special school or institution as referred to in Section 1 of the Dutch Primary Education Act (*Wet op het primair onderwijs*),

Section 1 of the Dutch Secondary Education Act (*Wet op het voortgezet onderwijs*), Section 1 of the Dutch Expertise Centres Act (*Wet op the expertisecentra*), Section 1.1.1. of the Dutch Adult and Vocational Education Act (*Wet educatie en beroepsonderwijs*) or Section 1.1. of the Dutch Higher Education and Research Act (*Wet op het hoger onderwijs en wetenschappelijk onderzoek*), and the reason for the termination lies in acts or omissions on the part of the employee that are incompatible with the identity of that school or institution arising from its religious or ideological basis, provided that consent for the termination was granted by an independent and impartial committee of the employer to which the rules referred to in Section 671a, paragraph 2, subparagraphs a to d apply mutatis mutandis.

2. The employee is entitled to revoke his/her agreement referred to in paragraph 1 within 14 days of the date thereof and without giving reasons based on a written declaration addressed to the employer.

3. If the employer does not refer the employee in writing to the right referred to in paragraph 2 within two working days of the agreement, the period referred to in paragraph 2 will be three weeks.

4. Insofar as agreement was required under paragraph 1 for a valid notice of termination, the notice of termination will be deemed not to have been given after a revocation as referred to in paragraph 2.

5. Paragraphs 2 to 4 do not apply if the employee once again agrees to the termination of the employment contract within six months of a revocation on the basis of paragraph 2 or a termination as referred to in Section 670b, paragraph 2.

6. Any stipulation by which the condition of written agreement as referred to in paragraph 1, or the right as referred to in paragraph 2, is excluded or limited is invalid.

Book 7, Section 671a

1. An employer who intends to terminate an employment contract on the basis of Section 669, paragraph 3, sub-paragraph a or b must request written permission for this purpose from the Employee Insurance Agency as referred to in Section 5 of the Dutch Work and Income (Implementation Organisation Structure) Act (*Wet structuur uitvoeringsorganisatie werk en inkomen*).

2. If an independent and impartial committee of the employer is appointed based on a collective labour agreement or a regulation made by or on behalf of a competent management body, the employer must, notwithstanding paragraph 1, request permission to give notice of termination of the employment contract from that committee on the basis of Section 669, paragraph 3, sub-paragraph a. The collective labour agreement or regulation made by or on behalf of a competent management body that designates this committee lays down rules relating to:

a. the principle of audi alteram partem;

b. the confidential handling of information submitted;

c. reasonable periods for responses from the employer and employee; and

d. a reasonable decision period.

3. The collective labour agreement as referred to in paragraph 2 is entered into with one or more employee associations whose members work in the company or business sector, whose object, according to their articles of association, is to protect the interests of their members as employees who are working as such in the company or business sector concerned, and that have had full legal capacity for at least two years. If an employee association may be deemed under its articles of association to be a continuation of one or more other employee associations with full legal capacity, the period of the full legal capacity of the other association(s) will be taken into account for determining the two-year period.

4. The decision on the request as referred to in paragraph 1 or paragraph 2 will be issued in writing simultaneously to the employer and the employee, stating the date on which the full request as referred to in paragraph 1 or paragraph 2 was received.
5. The consent to terminate an indefinite employment contract on the basis of Section 669, paragraph 3, sub-paragraph a will only be granted if the employer:
a. has terminated the employment relationship with people who are not employed on the basis of an indefinite employment contract in the jobs that have been made redundant;
b. has terminated the employment relationship with people who are employed on the basis of an employment contract as referred to in Section 628a in the jobs that have been made redundant; and
c. has terminated the contracts with hired personnel in the jobs that have been made redundant.
6. The consent for termination is valid for four weeks from the date of the decision on the request referred to in paragraph 1 or paragraph 2. The employer must give a written notice of termination that states the reasons for the termination.
7. Employment relationships or contracts for hired personnel to which paragraph 5 does not apply may be designated based on a regulation of the Minister of Social Affairs and Employment, which may also determine what is meant by employer under paragraph 5.
8. Rules relating to the procedure for granting permission as referred to in paragraph 1 may be laid down based on a regulation of the Minister of Social Affairs and Employment.
9. Any stipulation by which the obligation to request permission as referred to in paragraph 1 or paragraph 2 is excluded or limited is invalid, as is any stipulation that extends the period, as referred to in paragraph 6.

10. Rules relating to the committee, as referred to in paragraph 2, and the procedure for granting of permission by the committee may be laid down based on a regulation of the Minister of Social Affairs and Employment.

Book 7, Section 671b

1. The sub-district court may set aside an employment contract at the employer's request:
a. on the basis of Section 669, paragraph 3, sub-paragraphs c to h;
b. on the basis of Section 669, paragraph 3, sub-paragraphs a and b, if the consent, as referred to in Section 671a, is refused; or
c. on the basis of Section 669, paragraph 3, sub-paragraphs a and b, for fixed-term employment contracts that cannot be terminated early.
2. The sub-district court may grant the request referred to in paragraph 1 only if the conditions for terminating the employment contract as referred to in Section 669 have been satisfied and there is no prohibitions on termination as referred to in Section 670, or prohibitions on termination in another legal provision that are comparable with these prohibitions on termination in their nature and purport.
3. If the request for setting aside is based on Section 669, paragraph 3, sub-paragraph a, Section 671a, paragraphs 5 and 7 will apply mutatis mutandis.
4. If the request for setting aside is based on Section 669, paragraph 3, sub-paragraph c, the sub-district court will reject the request if the employer does not have an expert's statement as referred to in Section 629a.
5. If the request for setting aside is based on Section 669, paragraph 3, sub-paragraph e, in connection with the employee's failure without proper cause to comply with the obligations as referred to in Section 660a, the sub-district court will reject the request if the employer:

a. has not first given the employee a written demand to comply with those obligations or for that reason, and, with due observance of the provisions of Section 629, paragraph 7, has suspended the payment of wages; or
b. does not have a declaration relating to an expert as referred to in Section 629a, unless the submission of this declaration cannot reasonably be required of the employer.
6. If the employer requests the setting aside on the basis of Section 669, paragraph 3, sub-paragraphs b to h and a prohibition on termination as referred to in Section 670, paragraphs 1 to 4 and 10, or prohibitions on termination in another legal provision that are comparable with these prohibitions on termination by nature and purport apply, the sub-district court may grant the request for setting aside, notwithstanding paragraph 2, if:
a. the request does not involve circumstances to which the prohibitions on termination relate; or
b. there are circumstances of such a nature that the employment contract should be terminated in the employee's interest.
7. The prohibition on termination as referred to in Section 670, paragraph 1 does not apply if the illness commenced after the sub-district court received the request for setting aside.
8. If the request for setting aside relates to an indefinite employment contract or a fixed-term employment contract that can be terminated early, and the sub-district court grants the request:
a. it will set the end of the employment contract to the date on which the employment contract would have ended with normal notice of termination, whereby, if the setting aside of the employment contract is not the result of serious imputable acts or omissions on the part of the employer, the length of the period that commences on the date of receipt of the request for setting aside and ends on the date of the order for setting aside will be deducted, on the understanding that a period of at least one month remains;

b. it may, notwithstanding sub-paragraph a, set the end of the employment contract to an earlier date if the setting aside of the employment contract is the result of serious imputable acts or omissions on the part of the employee;
c. it may award reasonable compensation to the employee if the setting aside of the employment contract is the result of serious imputable acts or omissions on the part of the employer.
9. If the request for setting aside relates to a fixed-term employment contract that cannot be terminated early, and the sub-district court grants the request, it will set the date on which the employment contract ends, and:
a. it may award the employee compensation capped at the wage for the period that the employment contract would have lasted if it had ended by operation of law;
b. it may award the employee fair compensation, in addition to the compensation referred to in sub-paragraph a, if the setting aside is the result of serious imputable acts or omissions on the part of the employer; or
c. it may, if the setting aside of the employment contract is the result of serious imputable acts or omissions on the part of the employee, award the employer compensation capped at the wage for the period that the employment contract would have lasted if it had ended by operation of law.
10. Any stipulation by which the employer's possibility to request the sub-district court to set aside the employment contract as referred to in paragraph 1 is excluded or limited is invalid.

Book 7, Section 671c

1. The sub-district court may set aside the employment contract at the request of the employee due to circumstances of such a nature that the employment contract should end immediately or within the short term for reasons of fairness.

2. If the request relates to an indefinite employment contract or a fixed-term employment contract that can be terminated early, and the sub-district court grants the request:
a. it will set the date on which the employment contract ends; and
b. it may award reasonable compensation to the employee if the setting aside of the employment contract is the result of serious imputable acts or omissions on the part of the employer.
3. If the request for setting aside relates to a fixed-term employment contract that cannot be terminated early, and the sub-district court grants the request, it will fix the date on which the employment contract ends, and:
a. it may, if it seems fair to it under the circumstances, award the employee compensation capped at the wage for the period that the employment contract would have lasted if it had ended by operation of law;
b. it may award the employee fair compensation, in addition to the compensation referred to in sub-paragraph a if the setting aside is the result of serious imputable acts or omissions on the part of the employer; or
c. it may, if it seems fair to do so under the circumstances, or if the setting aside is the result of serious imputable acts or omissions on the part of the employee, award the employer compensation capped at the wage for the period that the employment contract would have lasted if it had ended by operation of law.
4. It may be stipulated based on a regulation of the Minister of Social Affairs and Employment that the sub-district court may set the compensation referred to in paragraph 3, sub-paragraph c at a higher amount if the employee performs a job in a business sector as designated in that regulation. Only jobs in a business sector designated in the ministerial regulation as referred to in Section 668a, paragraph 8 may be designated as a job referred to in the first sentence.

5. Any stipulation by which the employee's possibility to request the sub-district court to set aside the employment contract as referred to in paragraph 1 is excluded or limited is invalid.

Book 7, Section 672

1. Notice of termination is given with effect from the end of the month, unless a different date is designated based on a written agreement or common practice.
2. The notice period that the employer must observe when giving notice of termination is, for an employment contract that on the date of termination:
a. has lasted less than five years: one month;
b. has lasted five years or longer, but less than ten years: two months;
c. has lasted ten years or longer, but less than fifteen years: three months;
d. has lasted fifteen years or longer: four months.
3. The notice period that the employee must observe when giving notice of termination is one month.
4. If the permission referred to in Section 671a, paragraph 1 is granted, the notice period to be observed by the employer will be reduced by the length of the period that commences on the date on which the full request for permission was received and ends on the date of the decision on the request for permission, on the understanding that a period of at least one month remains.
5. The period referred to in paragraph 2 may be reduced only based on a collective labour agreement or a regulation made by or on behalf of a competent management body. The period may be extended in writing.
6. Derogation from the period referred to in paragraph 3 is possible in writing. If extended, the notice period for termination by the employee may not exceed six months, and, for the employer, may not be shorter than double that for the employee.

7. The notice period for termination referred to in paragraph 6, second sentence may be reduced for the employer based on a collective labour agreement or a regulation made by or on behalf of a competent management body, provided that the period is not shorter than that for the employee.
8. For the purpose of paragraph 2, employment contracts are deemed to form the same uninterrupted employment contract if they are reinstated in accordance with Section 682 or Section 683.
9. The party that gives notice effective from an earlier date than applies between the parties must pay compensation equal to the wage for the period that the employment contract should have continued had it been terminated by normal notice.
10. The sub-district court may reduce the compensation referred to in paragraph 9 if this seems fair to it under the circumstances, on the understanding that the compensation may not be less than the wage for the notice period as referred to in paragraph 2, or the wage for three months.

Book 7, Section 673

1. The employer owes the employee transitional compensation if the employment contract has lasted at least 24 months and:
a. the employment contract:
1. has been terminated by the employer;
2. has been set aside at the request of the employer; or
3. after it ends by operation of law, has not been consecutively renewed at the employer's initiative and no successive employment contract has been entered into before the end of the employment contract, which can be terminated early and commences after an interval of no more than six months; or
b. the employment contract, as a result of the serious imputable acts or omissions on the part of the employer:
1. has been terminated by the employee;

2. has been set aside at the request of the employee; or
3. after it ends by operation of law, has not been consecutively renewed at the employee's initiative.

2. The transition compensation for the first 120 months of the employment contract is equal to one-sixth of the monthly wage for every six-month period that the employment contract has lasted, and equal to one-quarter of the monthly wage for every consecutive six-month period. The transition compensation is capped at €75,000 or an amount equal to no more than twelve months' wages if this amount exceeds €75,000.

3. The Minister of Social Affairs and Employment alters the amount referred to in paragraph 2 with effect from 1 January each time, in accordance with developments in contract wages for the year in question, as estimated in the previous year and published in the Macro-Economic Surveys. The amount is also rounded off to the closest multiple of €1,000. The altered amount applies only if the employment contract ends or is not renewed on or after the date of the alteration.

4. For the purpose of calculating the term of the employment contract as referred to in paragraphs 1 and 2:
a. months in which average time of the work performed by the employee has not exceeded twelve hours a week, until reaching eighteen years of age is disregarded; and
b. one or more prior employment contracts between the same parties, which have followed each other by an interval of no more than six months, are added together. This also applies if the employee was successively employed at different employers that, regardless of whether there is insight into the capacity and suitability of the employee, must reasonably be deemed to be each other's successor with regard to the work performed.

5. If transition compensation is paid in the situation referred to in paragraph 4, sub-paragraph b upon the termination of a prior employment contract, or equivalent provision has been made on

the basis of Section 673b, paragraph 1, an amount equal to the transition compensation that was or would have been due in the event of termination on the basis of paragraphs 1 and 2 will be deducted from the transition compensation.

6. The following may be deducted from transition compensation under conditions to be determined by or pursuant to an order in council:

a. costs of measures relating to ending or not renewing the employment contract, aimed at preventing the unemployment or reducing the period of unemployment of the employee; and

b. costs relating to promoting the wider employability of the employee that have been incurred during the employment contract.

7. The transition compensation is not due if the employment contract ends or is not renewed:

a. before the date on which the employee reaches the age of eighteen and the average extent of the work performed by him/her does not exceed twelve hours a week;

b. in connection with or after reaching the age referred to in Section 7a, paragraph 1 of the General Old Age Pensions Act or a different age at which the employee's entitlement to pension arises; or

c. because of serious imputable acts or omissions on the part of the employee.

8. Notwithstanding paragraph 7, sub-paragraph c, the sub-district court may award all or part of the transition compensation to the employee if not awarding it would be unacceptable according to standards of reasonableness and fairness.

9. If an employment contract is not renewed after it ends by operation of law because of the serious imputable acts or omissions on the part of the employer, the sub-district court may:

a. award the employee fair compensation at the employer's expense, in addition to the transition compensation; or

b. if the employee has been employed at the employer as referred to in paragraph 1 for less than 24 months or is not entitled to transition compensation on the basis of paragraph 7, sub-paragraph a, award fair compensation to the employee at the employer's expense.

10. The meaning of wage for the purpose of paragraph 2 will be determined based on or pursuant to an order in council.

Book 7, Section 673a

1. If the employer is 50 years or older when the employment contract ends or is not renewed and the employment contract has lasted at least 120 months, the transition compensation for each six-month period that the employee has been employed at the employer after reaching the age of 50 is, notwithstanding Section 673, paragraph 2, first sentence, equal to half of the monthly wage as referred to in Section 673, paragraph 2.
2. Paragraph 1 does not apply to an employer that had fewer than 25 employees, on average, in the second half of the calendar year prior to the calendar year in which the employment contract ends or is not renewed.
3. Paragraph 2 does not apply to the categories of employees to be designated based on a regulation of the Minister of Social Affairs and Employment.
4. This section ceases to apply with effect from 1 January 2020.

Book 7, Section 673b

1. Sections 673 and 673a do not apply if an equivalent provision is included in a collective labour agreement or a regulation made by or on behalf of a competent management body as referred to in Section 673, paragraph 1 and Section 673a.
2. The collective labour agreement referred to in paragraph 1 is entered into with one or more employee associations whose members work in the company or business sector, whose object,

according to their articles of association, is to protect the interests of their members as employees who are working as such in the company or business sector concerned, and that have had full legal capacity for at least two years. If an employee association may be deemed under its articles of association to be a continuation of one or more other employee associations with full legal capacity, the period of the full legal capacity of the other association(s) will be taken into account for determining the two-year period.

Book 7, Section 673c

1. The transition compensation referred to in Sections 673, paragraph 2 and 673a, paragraph 1 is no longer due if the employer is declared insolvent, granted a moratorium on the payment of debts, or if the statutory debt management scheme for natural persons is declared applicable to it.
2. If payment of the transition compensation as referred to in Sections 673, paragraph 2 and 673a, paragraph 1 leads to unacceptable consequences for the employer's business operations, it may be paid in instalments under conditions to be determined based on a regulation of the Minister of Social Affairs and Employment. It may also be determined that the transition compensation will be increased by a percentage to be determined by that ministerial regulation.

Book 7, Section 673d

1. Notwithstanding Section 673, paragraph 2, months before 1 May 2013 may be disregarded for the purpose of calculating the term of the employment contract under conditions to be determined based on a regulation of the Minister of Social Affairs and Employment, if:
a. the employee was employed at an employer that had less than 25 employees, on average, in the second half of the calendar year

prior to the calendar year in which the employment contract ends or is not renewed; and

b. the employment contract ended due to circumstances as referred to in Section 669, paragraph 3, sub-paragraph a, resulting from the employer's poor financial situation.

2. This section ceases to apply with effect from 1 January 2020.

Book 7, Section 674

1. The employment contract ends on the death of the employee.

2. Nonetheless, the employer is obliged to pay his/her surviving relatives an amount equal to the last wage that the employee was entitled to from the date of his/her death until one month later.

3. For the purpose of this section, 'surviving relatives' means the surviving spouse or registered partners from whom the employee did not live separately on a permanent basis or those with whom the employee cohabited without being married; in the absence of these, it refers to the minor children with whom the deceased had a family relationship and, in the absence of these, those who lived with the employee in a family relationship and whose living costs he/she mostly funded. Unmarried cohabitation as referred to in the first sentence exists if two unmarried persons, with the exception of blood relatives in the first degree, run a joint household. A joint household as referred to in the second sentence exists if those involved have their principal place of residence in the same dwelling and demonstrate that they look after each other by making a contribution towards the costs of the household or providing for each other's care.

4. The death benefit referred to in paragraph 2 may be reduced by the amount of the payment that the surviving relatives are entitled to receive due to the death of the employee under statutory health or invalidity insurance and pursuant to the Dutch Supplementary Benefits Act (*Toeslagenwet*).

5. Paragraph 2 does not apply if the employee was not entitled immediately prior to his/her death, by virtue of Section 629 paragraph 3, to wages referred to in Section 629 paragraph 1, or was not entitled because of his/her actions to any payment under a statutory health or invalidity insurance.
6. Derogation from this section to the detriment of the surviving relatives is not possible.

Book 7, Section 675

The employment contract does not end because of the death of the employer unless the contrary is clear from the agreement. However, the heirs of the employer and the employee are entitled to give notice of termination of a fixed-term employment contract, with due observance of Sections 670 and 672, as though it were an indefinite employment contract. If the employer's deceased estate is divided in accordance with Section 13 of Book 4, the entitlement of the heirs as referred to in the previous sentence passes to the employee's spouse or registered partner.

Book 7, Section 676

1. If a probationary period has been stipulated, each of the parties is entitled, as long as the period has not expired, to give notice of termination of the employment contract with immediate effect.
2. If the employer terminates the employment contract, it must give the employee written reasons for the termination at his/her request.

Book 7, Section 677

1. Each of the parties is entitled to give immediate notice of termination of the employment contract for urgent cause, subject to notifying the other party of the reason without delay.

2. The party that has given the other party urgent cause through intent or fault to immediately terminate the employment contract is liable to pay the other party compensation if the other party exercises that right.
3. The compensation referred to in paragraph 2 is:
a. for an indefinite employment contract and a fixed-term employment contract that can be terminated early, equal to the wage for the period that the employment contract should have continued had it been terminated by normal notice;
b. for a fixed-term employment contract that cannot be terminated early, equal to the wage for the period that the employment contract would have lasted had it ended by operation of law.
4. If a party gives notice of termination of a fixed-term employment contract that cannot be terminated early, contrary to paragraph 1, compensation equal to the wage for the period that the employment contract would have lasted had it ended by operation of law will be payable to the other party. The sub-district court may reduce the compensation referred to in this paragraph if this seems fair to it under the circumstances, on the understanding that it may not be less than the wage for three months. The employee may request the sub-district court to nullify the notice of termination.
5. In relation to the compensation referred to in paragraph 2, the sub-district court may:
a. reduce it if this seems fair to it under the circumstances, on the understanding that the compensation referred to in paragraph 3, sub-paragraph a is at least equal to the wage for the period that the employment contract should have continued in accordance with the notice period as referred to in Section 672;
b. increase it, if the notice of termination is given by the employee and this appears fair to it under the circumstances.
6. It may be stipulated based on a regulation of the Minister of Social Affairs and Employment that the sub-district court may

set the compensation referred to in paragraph 4 at a higher amount, at the employee's expense, if the employee performs a job in a business sector as designated in that regulation. Only jobs in a business sector designated in the ministerial regulation as referred to in Section 668a, paragraph 8 may be designated as a job referred to in the first sentence.

7. Any stipulation by which the entitlement referred to in paragraph 1 is excluded or limited is invalid.

Book 7, Section 678

1. Such acts, characteristics or conduct of the employee, as a result of which the employer cannot reasonably be required to allow the employment contract to continue, constitute urgent cause for the employer to terminate the contract within the meaning of paragraph 1 of Section 677.

2. Urgent cause may be deemed to exist inter alia:

a. if the employee has misled the employer when entering into the employment contract by producing false or forged references, or having given intentionally false information about how his/her last employment contract ended;

b. if it turns out that the employee seriously lacks the competence or suitability for the work that he/she has undertaken to perform;

c. if the employee is drunk or guilty of other disorderly conduct, despite having been warned against it;

d. if the employee commits theft, embezzlement, fraud or other offences, as a result of which the employer's trust is betrayed;

e. if the employee mistreats, grossly insults or seriously threatens the employer or his/her family or household members;

f. if the employee tempts or tries to tempt the employer or his/her family or household members to perform acts that are contrary to the law or public decency;

g. if the employee intentionally or recklessly damages or exposes the employer's property to serious risk, despite having been warned against it;
h. if the employee intentionally or recklessly exposes himself/herself or others to serious risk, despite having been warned against it;
i. if the employee discloses details regarding the household or the business of the employer that ought to be kept confidential;
j. if the employee stubbornly refuses to comply with reasonable orders or instructions given to him/her by or on behalf of the employer;
k. if the employee grossly neglects the duties imposed on him/her by the employment contract in another way;
l. if the employee intentionally or recklessly becomes or remains incapable of performing the stipulated work.
3. Stipulations by which the decision of whether urgent cause within the meaning of Section 677, paragraph 1 exists is left up to the employer are invalid.

Book 7, Section 679

1. Such circumstances as a result of which the employee cannot reasonably be required to allow the employment contract to continue constitute urgent cause for the employee within the meaning of Section 677 paragraph 1.
2. Urgent cause may be deemed to exist inter alia:
a. if the employer mistreats, grossly insults or seriously threatens the employee or his/her family or household members, or tolerates that such acts are committed by one of the employer's household members or employees;
b. if the employer tempts or tries to tempt the employee or his/her family or household members to perform acts that are contrary to the law or public decency, or tolerates such temptation or

attempted temptation by one of the employer's household members or employees;
c. if the employer does not pay wages on the stipulated date;
d. if the employer does not duly provide any agreed board and lodging;
e. if the employer does not provide adequate work to the employee whose wage depends on the results of the work to be performed;
f. if the employer does not provide, or does not duly provide, the stipulated assistance to the employee whose wage depends on the results of the work to be performed;
g. if the employer grossly neglects the duties imposed on it by the employment contract in another way;
h. if the employer orders the employee, notwithstanding his/her refusal, to perform work in the business of another employer even though this is not inherent to the nature of the employment contract;
i. if the continuation of the employment contract would pose serious risks to the life, health, morality or good reputation of the employee that were not clear when the employment contract was concluded;
j. if the employee becomes incapable of performing the stipulated work because of illness or other causes beyond his/her control.
3. Stipulations by which the decision of whether urgent cause within the meaning of Section 677 paragraph 1 exists is left up to the employee, are invalid.

Book 7, Section 680a

The court is authorised to reduce a claim for continued payment of wages that is based on the voidability of the termination of the employment contract if awarding it under the given circumstances would lead to unacceptable results, although not to less than the wage for the duration of the notice period under Section 672 or less than the wage for three months.

Book 7, Section 681

1. At the request of the employee, the sub-district court may nullify the notice of termination of the employment contract by the employer or, at his/her request, award the employee fair compensation at the employer's expense, if:
a. the employer has given notice of termination contrary to Section 671;
b. the employer has given notice of termination contrary to Section 670, or prohibitions on termination in another legal provision that are comparable by nature and purport;
c. the employer has given notice of termination contrary to Section 646, 648 or 649, or any other prohibition on discrimination or in connection with the fact that the employee has relied, in or out of court, on Section 646, 648 or 649 or any other prohibition on discrimination or has granted assistance in that regard;
d. the employer, other than an employer as referred to in Section 690, arranges for another person to perform the same work that the employee performed before the termination of the employment contract, within 26 weeks of a notice of termination on the basis of Section 669, paragraph 3, sub-paragraph a and does not give the employee the opportunity to resume his/her previous work under the employer's normal conditions;
e. the employer as referred to in Section 690 fails when a vacancy arises for the same or comparable work as that performed by the employee before the employment contract was terminated within 26 weeks of termination on the basis of Section 669, paragraph 3, sub-paragraph a, to give the former employee the opportunity to put himself/herself forward as a candidate for the employment at the third party as referred to in Section 690.

2. Any stipulation by which the entitlement as referred to in paragraph 1 is excluded or limited is invalid.

Book 7, Section 682

1. At the request of an employee whose employment contract is terminated with the permission as referred to in Section 671a, the sub-district court may:
a. order the employer to reinstate the employment contract if the notice of termination was contrary to Section 669, paragraph 3, sub-paragraph a or b;
b. for a notice of termination contrary to Section 669, paragraph 3, sub-paragraph a, award fair compensation to the employee, at the employer's expense, if reinstatement is not possible because of a circumstance that amounts to a serious imputable act or omission by the employer; or
c. award fair compensation to the employee, at the employer's expense, if, due to circumstances referred to in Section 669, paragraph 3, sub-paragraph b, the notice of termination was the result of serious imputable acts or omissions on the part of the employer.
2. At the request of an employee as referred to in Section 671, paragraph 1, sub-paragraphs d or h, the sub-district court may:
a. order the employer to reinstate the employment contract if the notice of termination was contrary to Section 669; or
b. award fair compensation to the employee, at the employer's expense, if the notice of termination was the consequence of serious imputable acts or omissions on the part of the employer.
3. At the request of an employee as referred to in Section 671, paragraph 1, sub-paragraphs e or f, the court may award fair compensation to him/her, at the employer's expense, if the notice of termination:
a. was contrary to Section 669; or

b. was the consequence of the serious imputable acts or omissions on the part of the employer.
4. If the employer, other than an employer as referred to in Section 690, arranges for another person to perform the same work that the employee performed before the termination of the employment contract, within 26 weeks of the date of the order to set aside on the basis of Section 669, paragraph 3, sub-paragraph a, and has not given the employee the opportunity to resume his/her previous work under the employer's normal conditions, the sub-district court may, at the request of the employee:
a. order the employer to reinstate the employment contract with effect from the date on which it was terminated; or
b. award fair compensation to the employee, at the employer's expense.
5. If the employer as referred to in Section 690 fails when a vacancy arises for the same or comparable work as that performed by the employee before the employment contract was terminated, within 26 weeks of the date of the order to set aside on the basis of Section 669, paragraph 3, sub-paragraph a, to give the former employee the opportunity to put himself/herself forward as a candidate for the employment at the third party as referred to in Section 690, the sub-district court may, at the request of the employee:
a. order the employer to reinstate the employment contract with effect from the date on which it was terminated; or
b. award fair compensation to the employee, at the employer's expense.
6. If the sub-district court orders the reinstatement of the employment contract as referred to in paragraph 1, sub-paragraph a, or paragraph 2, sub-paragraph a, it will set the date on which the employment contract is to be reinstated and take measures regarding the legal consequences of the interruption of the employment contract.

7. Any stipulation by which the entitlement as referred to in paragraphs 1 - 5 is excluded or limited is invalid.

Book 7, Section 682a

Rules with regard to Sections 681, paragraph 1, sub-paragraphs c and d, and 682, paragraphs 4 and 5 may be laid down based on a regulation of the Minister of Social Affairs and Employment that may stipulate:

a. what is also understood by 'employer' under those Sections;
b. in which cases and under which circumstances those provisions are not applicable; and
c. in which order the previous employees will be given the opportunity to resume their previous work or to be put forward as candidates for employment.

Book 7, Section 683

1. If an appeal or appeal in cassation is lodged against an order to set aside the employment contract referred to in Sections 671b and 671c, or to nullify the notice of termination as referred to in Sections 677, paragraph 4, and 681, or for reinstatement of the employment contract as referred to in Section 682, this does not suspend the enforcement of the order.
2. Appeal and appeal in cassation against setting aside at the employee's request may relate only to the compensation referred to in Section 671c, paragraphs 2 or 3.
3. If the court finds on appeal or after referral in cassation that the employer's request to set aside the employment contract was granted incorrectly or that the employee's request to nullify the notice of termination or reinstate the employment contract was wrongly rejected, it may order the employer to reinstate the employment contract or award fair compensation to the employee.

4. If the court orders the reinstatement of the employment contract as referred to in paragraph 3, Section 682, paragraph 6, will apply mutatis mutandis.
5. If the court finds on appeal or after referral in cassation that the request of the employer or employee to set aside the employment contract was wrongly rejected, it will set the date on which the employment contract ends. Sections 671b and 671c apply mutatis mutandis to the award of compensation.
6. If the court finds on appeal or after referral in cassation that the employee's request to nullify the notice of termination or reinstate the employment contract was wrongly granted, it will set the date on which the employment contract ends.

Book 7, Section 684

1. If the employment contract was entered into for longer than five years or for the lifetime of a specific person, the employee is nevertheless entitled, from the moment five years since its commencement has passed, to give notice of termination thereof subject to a six-month period.
2. Derogation from this section to the detriment of the employee is not possible.

Book 7, Section 686

The provisions of this section do not exclude the possibility for either party to set aside the employment contract because of a failure to perform and to receive compensation. Only the court can order the setting aside of the employment contract.

Book 7, Section 686a

1. Statutory interest is due on the amount of the compensation referred to in Sections 672, paragraph 9 and 677, paragraphs 2 and 4, calculated from the date on which the employment contract ended. Statutory interest is due on the amount of the

transition compensation as referred to in Sections 673, 673a and 673c, calculated from one month after the date on which the employment contract ended.

2. Proceedings that are based on, by virtue of or pursuant to the provisions of this section are instituted based on an application.

3. In proceedings that are based on, by virtue of or pursuant to the provisions of this section, related claims may be instituted through an application.

4. The right to submit an application to the sub-district court ceases to exist:

a. two months after the date on which the employment contract ends, if:

1. the application relates to compensation as referred to in Sections 672, paragraph 9 and 677, paragraph 4; or

2. the application is on the basis of Sections 677, 681, paragraph 1, sub-paragraphs a and b, and 682, paragraphs 1, 2 and 3;

b. three months after the date on which the employment contract ends, if the application is on the basis of Sections 673, 673a, 673b, 673c and 673d;

c. two months after the date on which the employee is aware, or could reasonably have been aware, of the situation as referred to in Sections 681, paragraph 1, sub-paragraphs d and e and 682, paragraphs 4 and 5, but no later than two months after the date on which the 26-week period as referred to in those paragraphs or sub-paragraphs has expired;

d. two months after the date on which the permission referred to in Section 671a was refused, if the application is on the basis of Section 671b, paragraph 1, sub-paragraph b;

e. three months after the date on which the obligation on the basis of Section 668, paragraph 1 arose, if the application is on the basis of Section 668, paragraph 3.

5. The handling of the applications referred to in this Section commences no later than in the fourth week following that in which the application was submitted.
6. Before giving an order to set aside the contract as referred to in Section 671b or 671c to which compensation is attached, the court informs the parties of its intention and sets a period within which the applicant may withdraw the application. If the applicant does so, the court will only rule on the costs of the proceedings.
7. Paragraph 6 applies mutatis mutandis if the court intends to rule that the employment contract is to be set aside as referred to in Section 671b or 671c, without attaching the compensation requested by the applicant.
8. Section 55 of Book 3 of the Dutch Civil Code does not apply to Sections 677 and 681.
9. Applications on the basis of this section are made to the subdistrict court that has jurisdiction under Sections 99, 100 and 107 to 109 of the Dutch Code of Civil Procedure.
10. The court may split a case into two or more cases if the application and the claims submitted in the application as referred to paragraph 3 are not suitable for joint handling in the court's opinion. In the order for splitting, the court, insofar as relevant, specifies the additional court fee that will be levied on the parties under Section 8 of the Dutch Court Fees (Civil Cases) Act (*Wet griffierechten burgerlijke zaken*) and the period within which this court fee, or this increased court fee, must be paid. Split cases are continued according to their status at the time of splitting.